TEN 7

When Your Shift Ends
and Your Life Begins

Sheriff Mark Lamb (Ret)

Ten 7:
When Your Shift Ends
and Your Life Begins

Copyright 2025 by Mark T. Lamb

Published in the United States by BCG Publishing, 2025.
www.BCGPublishing.com

DISCLAIMER

The following viewpoints in this book are those of Mark T. Lamb. These views are based on his personal experience from his life and law enforcement and leadership career.

The intention of this book is to share his story about his public service career, his business life, and the things he has learned in that journey.

All attempts have been made to verify the information provided by this publication. Neither the author nor the publisher assumes any responsibility for errors, omissions, or contrary interpretations of the subject matter herein.

This book is for entertainment purposes only. The views expressed are those of the author alone and should not be taken as expert instruction or commands. The reader is responsible for his or her future action. This book makes no guarantees of future success. However, by following the values that are talked about in this book, the odds of having a successful business, law enforcement career, and life have a much higher probability.

Neither the author nor the publisher assumes any responsibility or liability on the behalf of the purchaser or reader of these materials.

The views expressed are based on the author's personal experiences within the business world, law enforcement profession, and everyday life.

I dedicate this book to all the amazing men and women
who serve in law enforcement, as first responders,
and in our military.

Thank you!

ACKNOWLEDGMENTS

Thank you to my beautiful wife, Janel, for all of the love
and support, and for being the amazing wife
and mother you are.

Thank you to my kids, Cade, Sadie, Cooper, Wyatt,
and Dayton, and to their awesome spouses, McKenna,
Zach, Caroline, and McKya. Love you guys!

I also love my grandkids,
Brody, Ivy, Elaine, Liberty, Cohen, and Jones.

CONTENTS

PART III
Leading Beyond the Line

"Ten 7"—The Call That Changed Everything

I was probably a mile out when I saw the flashing red and blue lights in the distance. I knew exactly what it meant.

I sat silently in the front passenger seat of my chief deputy's unmarked patrol vehicle. This was it. The moment had come. Less than a mile to go.

Eight years ago to the day—December 31, 2016—I was on my first patrol as the newly elected sheriff of Pinal County. Just a little over a month earlier, I had won my first election, and although I wouldn't officially be sworn in until midnight on New Year's Eve, I couldn't wait to hit the road.

I was the "new sheriff in town," and I was ready.

It had been a tough road getting to that night. Years of sacrifice, wins, losses, heartache, challenges, and triumphs. It hadn't just taken a toll on me, it had taken one on my wife and children. But we understood the importance of the path we had chosen to walk. Every hardship, every high and low made that first night in the passenger seat of my chief deputy's cruiser all the sweeter.

I sat there, quiet, reflecting on the journey ahead. It was a surreal moment. I knew God had delivered on His promises. Now it was time for me to deliver on mine. What did God have in store for me?

Fast-forward eight years—December 31, 2024. Tens of thousands of hours and thousands of experiences later, I found myself once again in the passenger seat. Once again riding beside my chief deputy and dear friend, Matt Thomas. And once again, I was quiet, overwhelmed with emotion as I reflected on the incredible journey God had taken me on.

As we turned onto the road leading into my neighborhood, I was stunned.

Patrol vehicles lined the street like sentinels. Deputies, posse members, and colleagues stood outside their cars in silence, saluting as we passed. The agency helicopter circled overhead, its spotlight casting a beam through the cold Arizona night—not just lighting up the street, but illuminating the road I had traveled for nearly a decade.

I had no idea they had planned this. It caught me completely off guard.

And then it hit me: I'd been a passenger this whole time. Only now could I see it clearly—it wasn't me who had been driving for the last eight years. It was God. I had just been along for the ride, doing my best to follow His lead.

As we rounded the corner toward my house, the floodgates opened.

There they were—my wife, Janel, our children, our grandkids—standing in front of our home, pride and tears on their faces. I couldn't even make eye contact. I felt like I was standing on an emotional landmine. One look, one word, and I would've broken down.

I gripped the mic. The same one I had used thousands of times to call out traffic stops, respond to critical calls, or check in during chaotic days.

But this time was different.

The words came slowly, heavy with meaning.

I took a breath. Steadied my voice. And made the call:

"Pinal 1... I just want to say thank you to all the dispatchers, the deputies, the detention officers, the employees, the posse, the COPs (Citizens on Patrol), and especially my command staff. Thank you for a great eight years. It's been an honor to serve with you. I love every one of you. I'm going to

miss you a ton. Pinal 1 signing off for the last time. Please show me Ten 7."

And that was it.

I stepped out of the patrol vehicle for the final time and embraced my wife. I kissed her. Then I hugged each of my kids and grandkids. One by one, I embraced every deputy, every member of my team who had shown up to honor the moment.

My heart was full.

That moment marked the close of one chapter. But it wasn't the end. It was the beginning of something new—a new patrol, a new beat, a new mission.

This book is for every man and woman who knows what it means to wear the badge, to serve under fire, to hold the line—and now stands at the threshold of what comes next.

Whether you're weeks from retirement, just starting to think about life outside the uniform, or already on the other side, wondering what your mission is now—this book is for you.

It's a guide. It's a road map. And it's a challenge.

Your shift might be over—but your calling isn't.

This is *Ten 7: When Your Shift Ends and Your Life Begins.*

PART I
The Shift Ends—
Leaving the Badge Behind

CHAPTER ONE

What's In Your Locker?

A reflection on what you've carried, packed, hidden, or ignored. Emotional baggage, skills, trauma, talents. This chapter invites readers to take inventory— personally and professionally.

Every lawman, first responder, or soldier knows the feeling: that quiet moment at the end of a long shift when you head into the locker room, or pop the trunk of your POV (Personally Operated Vehicle), or step through the door at home. You unzip your gear bag and hang up the uniform.

You take off your duty belt, remove the vest, and reach into your locker. Maybe there's a photo of your family taped to the inside. Maybe a pair of worn boots, or a coin from a tough case. Maybe nothing at all—just a cold metal box holding the tools of a life you've lived under pressure.

The truth is, that locker holds more than gear. It holds years of sacrifice. Missed birthdays. The weight of every hard call. It holds pride and pain. Brotherhood and betrayal. Lessons. Scars.

And when you retire—or even start thinking about it— that locker becomes something else. It becomes symbolic. A question:

What are you carrying out with you when you leave?

I remember the day I cleaned out my office.

Eight years. Two elected terms. What felt like a million miles of memories, and certainly thousands of miles on my boots.

It was quiet. I chose a weekend, when no one else would be around. Saturdays and Sundays at the sheriff's office are quiet—only dispatch was working, just down the hall from my third-floor office.

I wasn't sure how I'd feel packing it all up, so I chose solitude. Just me, the gear, and the gravity of the moment.

The shelves, the closet, and the space around me were filled with reminders. There were the decorations my wife picked out when I first moved in—plants, pictures, a Western theme that felt like home. There were small gifts and awards I'd received over the years, some from places as far away as Australia and Denmark.

On my custom cowhide leather-topped desk sat my engraved "American Sheriff" handcuffs and the matching knife. I had hundreds—maybe thousands—of challenge coins and patches from across the country.

In the closet: uniforms, equipment, memories.

In the drawers: letters. Some angry. Most supportive. All part of the experience.

And on the wall rack: my guns. Proudly displayed for eight years.

There was my Ruger .45 New Vaquero Cowboy pistol—gifted by a constituent and friend after I won my first election—resting snug in a black leather cowboy rig. And beside it, one of my most prized possessions: an engraved Henry .44-.40 lever-action rifle. A family heirloom now. A gift from my wife when I was sworn in as sheriff in 2017.

I worked through it all in silence—the kind of silence that feels heavy, final. When it was all packed, I just stood there.

That office had become a place where service, struggle, sacrifice, and appreciation had quietly piled up. Every item reminded me of the man I had been. But it also forced me to ask—who am I now?

I didn't walk out with just boxes. I carried the weight of every lesson, every failure, every victory, every gut instinct honed under pressure. A heart full of fire. A head full of hard-earned wisdom.

And I knew then—I wasn't finished. Just reassigned.

Most of us never stop to take inventory. We walk out the door carrying the same load we walked in with.

For some, that's a problem.

For others, that's potential.

This chapter is about opening your locker. Not just the one at the station, but the one inside your heart and mind. It's time to unpack the good, the bad, and the buried. Because if you don't know what you're carrying, you'll never know how to use it.

The Gear We Keep

Ask any veteran cop or soldier—they'll tell you some things never leave you.

You keep your sense of alertness. You hear radio tones in your sleep. You scan every crowd. You walk into a restaurant and face the door. Your spouse or significant other knows the drill by now. Those are not bad things though. The average citizen lacks self-awareness, let alone awareness of their surroundings.

I have often said that the average person has no idea just how close the wolves are to the door. Thanks to the military soldiers and the law enforcement in this country, most Americans sleep comfortably at night, never truly knowing the danger that surrounds them. We do! This awareness or heightened sense of security gives us an advantage.

In the business world our alertness may give us a slight edge on a potential opportunity or pitfalls. Our ability to recognize a bad situation can keep us from entering a bad business deal or hiring the wrong person. Our ability to scan a crowd and pick up on out-of-the-norm behavior will make us good at client recognition and customer service.

You also carry wisdom. Street smarts. Calm under pressure. A gut instinct you can't learn in a classroom.

The great philosopher Socrates said, "Mankind is made of two kinds of people: wise people who know they're fools, and fools who think they are wise."

Unfortunately, many people in society and in the business world are "fools who think they are wise." Institutional education is often viewed as more important or more valuable than streets smarts or the wisdom that comes from experience rather than a classroom. This is our advantage! Managing your business can be learned, but wisdom and street smarts can only be achieved through experience, failure, and consequences.

You've led people. Navigated high-stakes scenarios. De-escalated dangerous individuals. Made life-and-death calls in fractions of a second.

That's leadership. That's risk management. That's planning under pressure. That—whether you realize it or not—is entrepreneurship.

You might not see yourself as a businessperson, but you've been operating with a CEO mindset for years.

You just called it command presence.

The Stuff We Don't Talk About

Let's be honest—some of what's in the locker is pain. Hell, most of what's in our lockers is pain.

Trauma. Anger. Regret.

Maybe it's the call you couldn't forget.

My first police department was on an American Indian reservation. While the community was right on the edge of Mesa, Tempe, and Scottsdale, it was still a small community. That meant we often dealt with the same troubled souls. One specific call was particularly heartbreaking and traumatic. I will warn you this story may be triggering for so many of you first responders, police, and combat veterans, so if you do not want to read it, please skip over the next paragraph.

We were called to a residence in one of the community housing neighborhoods on the reservation, referencing three small children who were reported as being dead in the trunk of a car. The mother and her boyfriend had been drinking and were bothered by the children, so they disciplined them by putting the kids in the trunk of the vehicle. It was a hot Arizona day, so when the parents passed out in the house from drinking too much alcohol, it was fatal. They woke up hours later only to find the children dead in the trunk of the vehicle. The children were so desperate to get out that their little fingers left scratch marks on the inside of the roof of the trunk.

Who does that to their children? How do we, as first responders and military, process something like this? Who takes the memories and the pain of these types of calls from us? The truth is that nobody is taking the pain or erasing the memories of those experiences from us. We are left to deal with the trauma of calls like this and so many other calls.

Maybe it's the partner you lost.

Not long after I left my first agency to further my career as a deputy with the Pinal County Sheriff's Office, I received the tragic news that a friend had been shot and killed by one of the local gangsters who was known for being high on meth. The gang, which we had successfully disrupted and dismantled with a federal RICO case, wanted retribution on the cops for all the people we threw in prison. My friend pulled a traffic stop on one of the known vehicles driven by those gang members, but they never gave him a chance. The passenger immediately got out of the vehicle, raised an AK 47 rifle, and fired at the unmarked truck. The first bullet struck my friend in the head and he was gone.

How do we process that? How do the responding officers ever erase the memory of their slain friend and brother? How do we process the trauma and the anger? We will always ask ourselves, "What if I had been there to help my friend?"

Maybe it's the marriage that didn't survive the job.

I have been married to my amazing wife for over thirty years, and two-thirds of that was while I was a police officer and elected sheriff. While I have had marital success, my marriage is not the norm for police officers or military members. Unfortunately, the divorce rate for police officers and soldiers is above the national average. Whether it's the stress of the job, the trauma we experience, the shift work, the lack of sleep, the constant adrenaline ups and downs, or our supervisors, it is clear the toll our jobs can take on us and our families.

Maybe it's the kids who grew up while you worked nights and weekends or while you were deployed to some far-off developing country or combat zone.

Most of us have spent the better part of our careers working shift work. Many of us have been called out in the middle of the night to work. I have no doubt that, like me, you have also missed holidays, birthdays, school events, sports games, graduations, or moments where your kids just needed their mom or dad.

My wife and I were blessed with five kids. My middle son was a young boy when I started my career in law enforcement, and when I decided to run for sheriff, he was a teenager smack dab in the middle of the years where he needed his dad around the most. The community and my agencies got more of my time than he did, likely playing a major role in my son losing his way by hanging around the wrong people and getting into drugs. After many years of prayers, pleadings, heartaches, tragedies, and sleepless nights, my son, by the grace of God, turned his life around.

I couldn't help but partially blame myself for the years he was lost. Should I have been there for him more? If I had been there, would he have lost his way? How do we process the trauma of knowing that our jobs, our agencies, our teammates, and our communities have taken very valuable and sacred time away from our children?

These are just a few examples of the trauma and pains our paths of public service have brought us. We cannot erase them. We have to face them. Process them. Use them.

I love to read and I love a good movie. I especially love books and movies where a "hero" rises and saves the day. What you may not have noticed is what made that hero. If you think about all the heroes like Superman, Batman, Spiderman and so many others, they experienced a tremendous amount of loss, trauma, and pain. That's what made them heroes. They turned all those challenging and life-altering experiences into purpose. The villains in all those stories also went through the same type of traumatic experience, however they chose to let it fill them with hate, anger, and a desire to destroy and inflict their pain on others. The hero chose to use that pain as purpose to help others, to save others, to keep the world right and make it better.

Be the hero. Turn all those experiences, that pain, that trauma into purpose.

When people asked me how I processed all the terrible things I saw on duty, I'd usually joke, "I just put it in a closet in my brain."

You know the kind of closet. Stuffed to the gills. Overflowing with gear, grief, and things you'd rather forget. The only thing keeping it all from spilling into the hallway? A thin, shaking closet door.

"Don't open that door," I'd say. "Don't jiggle the handle. Don't even look at it."

However, here's the problem: You can't carry that baggage into your next mission.

You have to deal with it. Own it. Then use it.

That pain? It can weigh you down. Or it can become fuel.

I have a t-shirt that I have worn for years. My wife actually gets mad when I wear it because it's faded and there are tiny holes on the right side where the shirt rubs against the sights of my concealed Glock 34. I used to wear the shirt sometimes when I was speaking in front of large groups of people so that I could unbutton my black cowboy shirt during my speech to reveal the print on the front of the shirt. The shirt is black with the word SCARS in red lettering. On the stage I would explain to the audience why I loved the shirt so much. It also reminded me when I wore it that we all have scars. Some of the scars are physical. Some of the scars are emotional. Some of the scars are mental. Many people try to hide them; they don't want other people to see their scars. Maybe they are embarrassed by them. Maybe they think they are the only ones with those scars.

Here is what I love about my T-shirt. It's basically saying, "Wear your scars proudly." We all have scars, so don't be embarrassed by them. Own them. Scars are our way of showing everybody that whatever it was in life that tried to take us out, failed. We survived what life threw at us and we have the scars to prove it.

Wear your scars with pride.

You didn't go through all that for nothing. You were forged in fire. The best, most durable and useful tools are almost always forged in fire. Now it's time to take those lessons and tools—and build something new.

Time to Take Inventory

As you step into this next phase, I challenge you to ask yourself:

- What am I proud of from my years of service?
- What am I still holding on to that needs to be healed?
- What skills have I developed that I can use to build a business or serve others?
- What mission do I want to take on next?

Unpack your locker.

Be honest. Be bold.

Because your next assignment starts now.

CHAPTER TWO

The Badge Doesn't Make the Man

Letting go of identity tied to the uniform.
Learning to lead without authority or rank.

For years, when someone asked, "What do you do?"

I answered, "I'm the sheriff."

I wasn't always the sheriff.

Roughly twenty years ago I had a night that would change my life forever. Believe it or not, I did not start off wanting to be a police officer. As a matter of fact, I had never thought of being a police officer. Not as a kid, not as a teenager or as an adult. There were no police officers

in my family or my wife's family. It wasn't even on my radar. So how did I become a police officer, let alone a sheriff?

Oftentimes, we are what we see. Our upbringing plays a huge role in who we are in life. It doesn't mean we can't change the trajectory, but it certainly sets a familiar path.

My father was a businessman. All I knew throughout my life was owning your own businesses and being your own boss, and I was attracted to it. Many of the businesses my dad was involved in were international businesses. Places like the Philippines and Panama. I grew up seeing the risks that came along with entrepreneurship. The challenges, the rewards. The failures and the victories. As I watched my dad go through all of that, I knew I wanted to own my own businesses. So how did I become a police officer, a sheriff?

I spent most of the years in my twenties owning my own businesses. I worked for a few years as a herdsman on a dairy, a job I loved very much, but for the most part I was my own boss. I owned a concrete resurfacing company, a sales company, a paintball store, a landscaping company, and a pigeon control business. I had my share of difficult times and successful times, but I was doing what I wanted to do...right? So again, how did I become a police officer, let alone a sheriff?

When I was thirty-three years old, I was operating a fairly successful pigeon control business. I wasn't making a ton of money but I was consistently making decent money, month after month. When you own a business, it's often feast or famine, especially when you are a one-man operation, so the monthly consistency was nice. A major challenge of running a business alone is either you are spending your time selling the jobs or you are spending your time doing the jobs, and it's hard to balance that. The upside is you are still your own boss. Even though business wasn't bad, pigeon control was hard work, dangerous work, constantly being on pitched roofs or high ladders, and the worst part is, it was disgusting, dirty work cleaning up pigeon crap and nests.

More than all that there was something else that wasn't sitting right. I felt unsatisfied, unseen, and insignificant. Just didn't feel like I was achieving my potential in life. I was grateful to be blessed with the means to support my family, but I longed for a greater purpose.

I had a neighbor and friend named Scott who was a police officer at a nearby American Indian reservation. I always loved hearing the crazy stories he would tell us when he came over to watch UFC fights at my house or when we would see each other leaving or coming home from work. I think he could see that I wasn't excited or fulfilled with what I was doing. I also think he could clearly see I was looking for purpose, and I will be grateful to him forever for seeing that.

One day Scott asked me to do a ride-along with him. A "ride-along" is where civilians can ride with an officer or deputy to see what police work is like firsthand. To be honest I wasn't super interested in doing a ride-along, but I also didn't have any reason to tell him no, so I agreed.

He worked graveyard shift on an American Indian reservation, so who knew what we might encounter. I don't remember much from that night, except for one call.

We responded to a call involving a dad who had found his fourteen-year-old daughter with a twenty-year-old man in their home. As you might imagine, the dad and the suspect got into a little scuffle in the house, and the suspect ran out of the back and into the desert area behind the residence. We arrived shortly after and commenced looking for the suspect. Normally on a ride-along the officer or deputy would have you wait in the vehicle on a call like this, but thankfully my friend let me join in the fun!

So there I was, out in the desert of the American Indian reservation where my friend worked, armed with a flashlight and courage. While out in the desert, I noticed a small abandoned travel trailer. My gut told me he had to be in there. I slowly walked up to the trailer and looked through the broken window. The trailer was full of trash and old clothes, but as I looked closer, I saw what I thought was a quarter size of skin hiding underneath a pile of trash and old clothes. I signaled to the officers and got their attention, then pointed into the travel trailer and mouthed, "I think he's in here." The officers made their way into the trailer and immediately found the suspect hiding under all of the trash and clothes. They dragged him out of the travel trailer, tasered him, and put him in cuffs. My heart was racing, and I immediately knew I needed more of this.

That morning when I got home, I woke up my wife and told her I was going to be a cop. My life was going to change! Within six months of my ride-along I was hired and getting ready to start the police academy. I had just turned thirty-four years old and I felt that I had found the purpose I was looking for. I had found my answer.

Twenty years later, that badge I had worked so hard for, the badge I wore every day, the badge I found so much purpose in, was now coming off. That answer I found and lived for two decades wasn't there anymore. Suddenly I wasn't "Pinal 1" on the police radio or Sheriff

Lamb in the press conference. I was just Mark. A husband. A father. A grandfather. A man with worn-out boots, scars on his heart, and a longing for new purpose in his head.

Who am I *now*?

Losing the Badge, Finding the Man

It happens to all of us. One day, you're putting on the uniform like armor—feeling the weight of duty, the authority of the badge, the purpose it gives you. Then retirement comes. The last watch ends. The radio goes quiet.

And that silence? It can be deafening.

Too many good men and women fall apart in that silence. They become ghosts in their own homes. Wandering through life, wondering why they feel lost, aimless, or like they left the best part of themselves behind in a cruiser or a combat zone. This is normal and you are not alone.

Here's what you need to know, something I had to remind myself of:

The badge didn't *make* me or you. It just revealed to us what was already inside. Courage. Discipline. Honor. Grit. The uniform and the badge may come off, but the man remains.

A Story: The Day After

The morning after I signed off "Ten 7," I didn't set an alarm. Granted, it was New Year's Day, but I still wouldn't have set an alarm. After years of shift work, graveyard shifts, call outs, or waking up before the sun, I figured I'd sleep in. Funny how your body doesn't forget the schedule. I was still up early, energy drink in hand, sitting there, wondering what this new day, this new year would bring.

But something felt...off.

I didn't have any briefings or meetings or community events to get to. No radio traffic in my ear. No take-home vehicle parked in my driveway. While I was getting a ton of "happy New Year" texts and congratulatory texts on a great career, I wasn't getting any texts or emails about crazy calls from the night before, citizen complaints, or media inquiries. Nothing, nada, zilch. I suddenly felt disconnected.

Just eight hours earlier I was in charge of 600 employees, 500,000 people, a county the size of Connecticut, a $60 million budget—and just like that, I wasn't.

And while I was excited for new opportunities, for a moment—I'll be honest—I felt less important.

That thought hit me hard. Because for years, being "sheriff" wasn't just a job title. It was who I was. The decisions, the pressure, the responsibility—I wore it like a second skin, but that morning, like so many times before, God again whispered something different into my heart: Your purpose isn't attached to a title. It's in your soul. You can hang up the uniform and gear, you can put the badge in a drawer and the gun on your nightstand. However, your ability to lead, to serve, to impact lives—that never goes away. You just need to shift where you point that ability.

You need to change how you use those hard, experience-earned talents you have acquired throughout your career.

Defining Yourself on Your Own Terms

So who are you when no one's calling you sergeant? When there's no uniform to wear or orders to follow? No policy manual telling you how to operate or what you can or cannot do. It may be a new or strange situation, but it is truly liberating. You don't need a supervisor or a set of policies to tell you the right thing to do. You know what to do!

You're still a protector. A leader. A warrior with wisdom. You earned those titles and gifts—they're yours. Now you're free to use those gifts in a new way—your way, on your terms. No bad supervisors to get in your way or ruin your day. Just you. You get to set the vision, the work environment, the game plan...it's all you. You can build something.

A business. A brand. A legacy. There are few things more satisfying than building something that allows you to leave your stamp on this world. You can lead your family deeper. Our families deserve our attention and leadership.

Entering the world of entrepreneurship and business ownership can give you the freedom and resources to spend quality time with your family. Developing a business that can involve your family is also rewarding.

You can mentor the next generation.

When I retired as sheriff, I knew I wanted to build some businesses with my wife and kids. I also knew my kids had been on the back burner for so many years, and I had not dedicated the time to mentoring my own children in being entrepreneurs and business owners. This was my opportunity. I knew that initially it would impact my wife's income, but it was the perfect time to mentor my kids and make them creators and partners in our business ventures. While I can't always recommend doing business with family, I think working with your children can be extremely gratifying. There is an inherent trust with your children. As a parent, you should always want your kids to be better than you.

You can serve your community in a way you never had time for before.

Over the last couple decades, I have been able to serve my community as a police officer, as a deputy, and as an elected sheriff. I wouldn't trade those experiences for anything. However, now I have the opportunity to serve in a different way. As first responders or soldiers, we don't usually get to choose our opportunities to serve, and we don't always get to deal with the best society has to offer. As an entrepreneur, you can now decide how you will serve your community, on your terms. You also have the time and freedom to serve the way you want. I truly believe that giving back, serving others, and being a good citizen are critical for success.

First, you have to separate your *identity* from your *rank*. You have to remind yourself that your value isn't tied to a badge number, a radio call sign, or a title on a door.

One of the hardest things to accept when leaving our professions is that "the show goes on." We invest so much of our lives into our careers, and then we are confronted by the harsh reality that the day after we walk away or retire, our agencies don't skip a beat. They turn off our email, they throw our badges in a box, they give our equipment to somebody else, and they backfill our positions. It feels wrong! Somewhat anticlimactic. What did we expect though? Did we think everything would shut down? No, but I think we wanted to know we meant more to the profession than just being a number. This is why I advise first responders and military not to stay too long. Save some of those years for you, for your family, for your business.

Here is the truth: Your value is eternal. God-given. Battle-tested. Proven.

From Chain of Command to Chain of Purpose

When you wore the uniform, your path was laid out: academy, patrol, promotion. Now the path is yours to forge.

It's both a blessing and a burden.

There's no one telling you what to do next. No ops plan. No commanding officer. That's scary to some—but it's also your greatest freedom.

One of the reasons I decided to run for sheriff was because I could see there was a lack of true leaders in our professions. The majority of the men and women in supervisory positions in the military, law enforcement, and fire are not leaders, they are supervisors. In most cases those supervisors got to where they are because they had the time on the job and they tested well, but they didn't inspire others to follow. Stripes on their sleeves or bars and stars on their collar does not make them leaders. I wanted to change that. I wanted not only to inspire those whom I was asked to lead, but I also wanted to mentor and prepare men and women who would be leaders.

Now you will have your chance to be the leader for your family and your business. You are the boss. You are in charge. This is your ship.

This is where the *entrepreneur's beat* begins.

You get to call the shots. Build the plan. Take the risk.

You become the one whom other people will look to and say, "*I want* to follow that guy." But before you can lead anyone else, you've got to lead yourself.

Checkpoint: Redefine Yourself

Take a moment right now to answer these questions honestly:

- If I couldn't say what I *used* to do, how would I describe who I *am*?
- What do I love doing that has nothing to do with law enforcement or military service?
- What kind of legacy do I want to leave for my kids or grandkids?
- If I could start over today, what would I build?

Good news, you're not starting over empty. You're starting over with some really useful business skills, like experience, wisdom, and the strength to build something that lasts. And the best part: There is nobody there to screw it up or stop you.

CHAPTER THREE

Lessons from the Field

What years on the street or in the field taught you about people, pressure, risk, and responsibility— and how those are business assets.

There's something that happens when you've spent years in the field—your brain rewires itself. You start to pick up on things others miss. You read people before they open their mouths. You notice tension in the air before it ever escalates. You hear what isn't said. You feel the mood of a room before you cross the threshold.

It's instinct. A sixth sense. And it's not taught in any classroom or university. It's forged.

In squad cars at 2 a.m. In chaotic homes filled with shouting and fear. On roadside traffic stops, where backup is twenty minutes out. In courtrooms, jail cells, and war zones.

And here's the thing: Those instincts don't retire when the badge comes off. In fact, they become your *greatest assets*.

The Edge You Didn't Know You Had

Let's break it down.

You've had to:

- Manage time, chaos, and logistics every single day.
- Lead people under pressure—sometimes with lives on the line.
- Talk to everyone from politicians and attorneys to criminals and victims.
- Communicate clearly, calmly, and confidently while your heart pounds.
- Be held accountable by the public, the press, and your chain of command.
- Stay composed under scrutiny, risk, and second-guessing.
- You've "sold" people on a traffic ticket or into handcuffs.

You've developed skills most business schools don't even know how to teach.

Now ask yourself: What entrepreneur wouldn't want that kind of training? While they're reading books on leadership, you've *lived it*. While they're practicing crisis management through hypothetical case studies, you've managed actual crises. While they're learning negotiation tactics in seminars, you've de-escalated armed suspects in back alleys and living rooms.

You don't lack business experience, you've just called it by different names.

A Story: The Traffic Stop That Taught Me Everything

Over the years I have pulled thousands of traffic stops. Whether I was dealing with gang bangers during my time as a gang and drug detective on the reservation, or as a sheriff pulling traffic stops on human trafficking and drug trafficking load vehicles or just some random vehicle, you rely on your training and your gut instinct to keep you safe.

I remember one traffic stop when I pulled over a vehicle on the reservation. It was late, dark, and backup wasn't close. Two young men were inside the vehicle. I was familiar with both of them because they belonged to one of the violent reservation gangs we were doing a federal RICO case on. The driver was somewhat calm, but the passenger was twitchy. Wouldn't make eye contact. My gut was on high alert. These guys were known to carry guns as well.

While running their info, I chatted—not friendly conversation but familiar. I was calm but probing. Like most gang bangers, they weren't as chatty. What I was really doing was assessing the situation.

And then I saw it. A tiny shift.

His body language changed. His hands started to get restless, moving toward the door. This is where the years of training and experience makes all the difference. You've seen it before so many times. A slight movement in their body that says they are going to run or reach for something.

We are always taught, "Watch the hands." It's the hands that can hurt you. Whether it's the hands attempting to strike you, the hands reaching for something, or the hands moving to open the door—whatever it is, WATCH THE HANDS.

His face, his eyes, his hands, his body, they were all sending me messages. The average citizen or businessman wouldn't have picked up on any of this. I did.

I stepped back, hand near my weapon. Calm but clear. More bass in my voice now. "Don't do it. Keep your hands where I can see them."

He froze. I had read him right.

The bass in my voice, my calmness, and my body language were telling him this was not going to go well for him. He knew I was in command of this situation.

Turns out, he had a weapon tucked under the seat and a felony warrant. That stop could've gone very wrong, but instincts, composure, command presence, and training turned potential disaster into control.

That moment and so many other traffic stops and calls for service have taught me a powerful truth: **You don't need to know everything. You just need to trust what you've trained.**

In business, that same lesson applies.

You'll face shady deals. Vendors who don't deliver. Clients who test your patience. Deadlines that feel impossible. The skills that kept you alive in the field? They'll keep your business strong.

The trained and learned skills you have acquired in your careers have prepared you for the business world. They have prepared you for success in business. They have prepared you for dealing with people, for sales, for reading situations, for recognizing the slightest changes in behaviors or conditions that the average entrepreneur may not ever be able to master.

Our job at Ten 7 is to help you transition those skills into not only business ownership, but also into success in the next chapter of your life.

From Squad Room to Board Room

Let's translate it further.

- **Briefings** become business meetings.
- **Case files** become customer profiles.
- **Operational plans** become launch strategies.
- **After-action reports** become debriefs and performance reviews.

Briefings. I'm sure the word "briefing" for many of us makes us glitch. I remember so many of those briefings, after my sergeant would pass on all the new administration BS to us line-level guys, where we left thinking, *Why am I doing this job?* The truth is the briefings were supposed to be, and usually were, the opportunity to get on the same page as a squad. We would discuss the mission and priorities of the shift.

Business is the same. Whether it's a daily or weekly or monthly meeting, the business meeting, or briefing, is where you get your team on the same page. To discuss the daily or weekly goals. To discuss the successes of the previous days or weeks. You are professionals at this. Now all we do is adjust from a briefing mindset to a business mindset. The best part? You are in charge and you get to set the mission and the tone.

Case Files. As first responders and military, we tend to be adrenaline junkies. The more dangerous the call, the more we love it. The worst part is usually the paperwork. For a few minutes of fun, we spend hours documenting what we did. We put case files together. Believe it or not, this will help you as an entrepreneur. You are already proficient in customer profiles, noting details about your customers and the work you did. The best part is that the customer profile will be much less paperwork than a case file, and hopefully far more lucrative.

Operational Plans. These were an important part of our success. Unlike in business, the stakes of having a good operational plan in law enforcement or military was a matter of life or death. Our goal was to make sure we executed the operation, the search warrant, the manhunt in a safe and efficient manner so nobody got hurt and we all made it home. Operational plans were an extremely important part of success. They are just as important in business as they are in our worlds. Putting together and executing a good business strategy, or operational plan, for a business launch, marketing strategy, new product announcement, etc., will make or break the success of your business. Just like an operational plan, it can be the difference between life and death. The good news is you are seasoned operational planners. If you apply the same attention to detail to your business strategies, you will be successful.

After-action Reports. Understanding what we did wrong and right in every operation, call, major incident, or battle is an important part of what we do. Hardly anything ever goes perfectly, no matter how much you plan. And sometimes the things you planned to do, even if well executed, turn out to have been the wrong thing to do. This is the purpose of after-action reports.

Business is no different. Sometimes things can go very right, sometimes they can go very wrong, and sometimes they go exactly as planned, but it still went wrong. Debriefs and performance reviews allow us to take an account of the things that went well, the things that didn't, what plans worked, and which ones could have been better. Sometimes it was a great plan poorly executed, while sometimes it was a plan perfectly executed, but it turned out to be a bad plan. Your firsthand on-the-job experience with after-action reports makes you a great fit for business debriefs and performance reviews. Whether it's a new business launch, a marketing strategy, or a new product release, your candid, no-nonsense approach will allow you to methodically assess the failures and successes of your business. You will be the best asset to your business.

In the field, you also made decisions under pressure, documented your actions, managed personnel, and adjusted strategies in real time.

That's business.

You just did it wearing a vest, tactical gear, or a uniform instead of a suit.

Emotional Intelligence of Warriors

People love to paint first responders and veterans as tough, hardened, stoic. And sure, we are. However, the truth is, the best among us are emotionally intelligent.

We've had to be.

We learned how to calm a panicked child, earn the trust of a terrified victim, or talk a suicidal veteran off a ledge. We learned when to speak—and when silence had more power.

That emotional range? That balance of strength and empathy?

It's not soft. It's *strategic*.

In business, it's how you build loyal clients. How you keep a team together. How you negotiate with integrity. How you lead without barking orders.

The best leaders aren't just commanding, they're compassionate. And you've had years of practice.

Another Story: The House Call That Rewired My Thinking

There was a domestic call I responded to early in my career. A husband had lost his job and taken it out on his wife—verbally, not physically.

I separated them. Listened to both. Calmed the storm.

When I sat with the man, I didn't lecture. I didn't scold. I just asked questions. Listened. Gave him room to speak.

He broke down. Not out of guilt—out of fear. He felt like a failure. Like his identity had been stripped away with that job.

That moment stuck with me. While I felt for that man because of the fear and uncertainty he was feeling, I was sadder for him that he had allowed his identity to be tied to and defined by a job. His fate and the security of his family were tied to the control and authority that his job and supervisors held over him. They had paid him just enough to keep his family above water, maybe a vacation each year if they planned well, but he wasn't the master of his fate. He was a passenger on somebody else's ship. Had he owned his own business, he still may have had some of the same stresses and fears, but he would have been the master of his fate.

As somebody who has always owned his own businesses, I made a decision that I would never let my career or job be in control of my fate. I also wanted to make sure others in my profession would never feel that fear or uncertainty either.

Years later, now that I have left law enforcement, I want to help you. You might be facing retirement. You may still be on the job but struggling with inflation and an increasingly difficult economy. You may have stepped away into retirement. Whatever your circumstance, like that man, you may be feeling fear and uncertainty.

Maybe you are asking yourself, "Who am I without the job?" "What do I do if I'm not the man in charge?"

I can honestly say I don't miss most aspects of being in law enforcement. I miss working with the guys. I miss being the decision-maker. I miss the adrenaline spikes. I miss being Sheriff Lamb. While I may be Ten 7, I am still the master of my fate.

You don't need the job to dictate who you are or how much you make. You don't need someone telling you what to do. You don't need to be in charge. You DO need to be the master of your fate.

This is the purpose of *Ten 7*. I want to help all of you take control of your life. I want you to be the master of your fate. I want you to be a successful business owner.

All of that emotion. All of that empathy. All of those calls for service—that ability to see through the surface—is what helps you not just *run* a business but build one that matters.

Checkpoint: Tactical Lessons for Business

Ask yourself:

- What was one of the toughest decisions I ever made under pressure? What did it teach me?
- How have I managed failure? What strengths came out of it?
- What leadership qualities did I earn the hard way—on the job?
- What instincts do I trust now that didn't come from a textbook?

These aren't just war stories or patrol memories. They're the *foundation* of your business resume.

You've already been tested. Now it's time to *redeploy*.

CHAPTER FOUR

Purpose Doesn't Retire

*Why your mission never ends—
only the method of service changes.*

Somewhere along the line, we were sold a lie: that retirement is the finish line. That it's the day you step off the field, hang up the uniform, and fade quietly into the background. We were led to believe we would have the money to ride off into the sunset and live a great life.

That may work for some folks. But not for warriors.

For those of us who've worn the badge or a uniform, carried the weight of responsibility, or stood a post far from home, purpose isn't just something we clocked in for. It's something etched into our bones.

We need purpose. And when the job ends, the purpose doesn't.

It just shifts.

You Were Built for More

If you're reading this, chances are you're not looking for a rocking chair and daytime TV. You're not wired to sit still. You've spent a career showing up early, staying late, answering the call when others ran the other way.

So what now?

Here's the truth: You're not retired. You're "redeployed."

You've got wisdom, leadership, instincts, and a fire in your gut that hasn't gone out. You have lived through danger, sacrifice, service, and command. And while your uniform may be hanging in the closet, your mission isn't.

The world still needs what you've got—your community, your family, and maybe even the business you're about to build.

For the last eight years I had the honor of serving as the sheriff of Pinal County. While I had a few months to come to terms with my retirement from law enforcement, I knew things would change. I still wanted to play a role. To have an impact.

I had been blessed to be in a position to develop the talents God gave me. As a sheriff, I was able to have a major impact in my community, state, and across the country. I was in a position of leadership, not just in my agency and county, but as a national leader in law enforcement. I had been a common sense, national voice for God, family, freedom. I refused to lose that in retirement.

I immediately started seeking opportunities that would allow me to continue to be a leader. To continue to be a strong voice. I would use my business to stay active working with companies and organizations that were engaged in important issues and law enforcement.

My mission changed. The battlefield was different. I was no longer sheriff, but my leadership and voice would continue on.

The Crisis of Quiet

I've spoken with a lot of good men and women who thought they were ready for retirement.

And for the first few weeks, it feels like you finally made it. You sleep in. You get to those projects around the house. You take your spouse to dinner without checking your radio. You hit the lake.

But then, it creeps in.

The silence.

That subtle, unsettling restlessness. Like the world is moving on without you. Like you're on the sideline watching a game you used to play.

For some, that turns into boredom. For others, depression. And for many, it turns into a slow fade—a soft, invisible slide into irrelevance.

But here's what I'll tell you straight: You were not created to go quietly. You were created to lead boldly.

Did you know that several studies, including a study from the Office of Justice Programs, have shown that the average police officer dies within five years after retirement? That our post-retirement life expectancy is twelve years less than the average citizen? The leading cause of death for retired police officers is heart disease. Years of shift work, bad sleep, adrenaline spikes and dumps, energy drinks, coffee, poor eating habits, stressful situations, and much more are contributing factors.

Unfortunately, suicide is also an alarming trend among police officers and military veterans.

I hate to share these types of statistics. I don't want to be a downer. I want to be a truth speaker. I want you to live. I want to help change those statistics.

We need purpose. We need a reason to keep challenging ourselves. We need a reason to keep contributing. We need a reason to continue to train and become masters of our craft.

We need to be entrepreneurs. We need to keep moving forward with purpose.

A Story: A Conversation That Lit a Fire

Not long after I stepped down as sheriff, I attended a leadership event in Texas.

I sat with a retired Marine who had done three tours, led men into battle, and carried the weight of command.

I asked him, "How are you doing in retirement?"

He looked me in the eye and said, "I thought I was done. I thought I had served my purpose. But now I realize I'm just getting started. I may not wear the uniform anymore, but the mission never leaves you. I just had to find a new battlefield."

That hit me like a freight train.

Because that's exactly it.

The mission doesn't end. It evolves.

The Ten 7 Transition

When you make your final radio call—your Ten 7—it marks the end of one assignment. But not the end of your duty.

You don't leave behind the mindset, the leadership, the strength, or the instincts.

You carry them forward.

Your Ten 7 isn't final. You're not riding off into the sunset. It's a shift. You're stepping off the radio frequency and onto a new channel.

One where *you* choose the mission.

Your Next Mission: Ownership

You've always served someone else's mission—your department, your agency, your country.

Now it's time to serve your own.

For years, as a police officer, a detective, a deputy, and a sheriff, I spent tens of thousands of hours serving. I served the communities. I served the men and women I led. I served God. I served my country. As have you. I wouldn't have changed any of it. All those hours, days, nights, months, and years serving were always about serving somebody else. It's time to shift.

Now we serve our mission. It still requires we serve others, but it's on our terms. Now we are building businesses that will bring value to our customers, our communities, and more importantly, our families and ourselves.

What does that mean?

That might mean:

- Starting a business
- Mentoring the next generation
- Launching a nonprofit
- Building a brand
- Buying land or investing in your community
- Writing a book, starting a podcast, or speaking your truth

The form doesn't matter. The leadership behind it does. The purpose does.

You don't need permission anymore.

You're the commanding officer now.

Redeploy with Intent

This new mission is about freedom, but also responsibility. You have been given and acquired experiences, tools, and credibility that others haven't.

And the world *needs* what you have.

So many people in this world are lost. They lack purpose. They are easily manipulated by other people or the news or social media. They struggle with self-worth or identity. They have no idea how to resolve conflict. They are entitled. They justify their worth by attacking others.

Our careers and experiences can make us jaded and direct. That can often lead us to be perceived as jerks or a**holes. We're not, we have just seen the world through a completely different lens. We have encountered evil eye to eye and battled with it. We have faced the monsters who prey on others. We have seen death and had to deal with the grief it leaves behind. We have been marriage counselors. We have been saviors. We have been hated. We have been loved. We have been villains. We have been heroes. We *are* heroes.

Because of everything we have seen, experienced, and been through in our careers and lives, we are different than the majority of the population. Our talents and abilities make us unique. We stand out. The confidence and command presence we exude, which is second nature to us, makes people feel uncomfortable or even scared when they are around us. Sometimes that can make us feel like lions in a field full of sheep. That's not the worst thing. We are lions: we are confident, and we know how to command a situation. But now we have to learn to use that confidence and command presence as an asset.

Instead of making people feel uncomfortable or scared, we use our valuable skills to make them feel at ease with our confidence that we will deliver a quality product or service and we will be in command of the job no matter what may arise.

You have an impressive set of skills, skills that many will never be able to acquire in a lifetime of business. Not only can you use them to build a successful business as an entrepreneur, you can share what you have learned.

You can give wisdom to younger men and women just entering the fight. You can offer leadership in a time when real leaders are hard to find. You can build something that brings your family together—and helps them prosper.

The Danger of Drifting

If you don't claim your new mission, the world will give you distractions.

The couch. The news. The comfort of doing nothing.

Nobody is immune from the distractions and comforts that life will throw at you. The difference is discipline and courage.

Discipline will get you up in the morning and out of that warm, comfortable bed. Discipline will get you in the gym, regardless of whether you feel like it or not. Discipline will keep you eating a healthy diet. Discipline will make you set your goals and achieve them every day. Discipline will drive you to continue to train. Discipline will condition you to make the calls. Discipline will keep you moving forward, even when things aren't going your way. You will need discipline to be a successful entrepreneur and business owner.

Courage will push you past your fear. Courage will get you to make the decision to start that business. Courage will get you to submit the retirement paperwork. Courage will take an idea and make it a reality. Courage will be what you use to make the calls. Courage will help you share your dreams and passions with the world. You will need courage to build a successful business or brand.

Oh yeah, you'll need *grit* too. I'd like to tell you every day as an entrepreneur will be easy, but I'd be lying. That's where the grit is needed.

University of Pennsylvania psychology professor Angela Duckworth, TED speaker and author of the book *Grit: The Power of Passion and Perseverance,* did a study on grit. What her study showed is that among all of the attributes, grit was the most important for success. I love this because it tells me you don't have to be the most talented or the smartest person, you just have to have a ton of grit to be successful. Luckily, you already have it.

We were built for purpose. For direction. For movement.

That's why it's so important to step into Ten 7 with clarity. With vision. With a sense of where you're going, not just where you've been.

Checkpoint: Define Your Purpose

Grab a notebook. Be brutally honest:

- What fires you up right now?
- What problem in the world do you feel called to solve?
- What do people come to you for help with?
- If money weren't an issue, how would you spend your time?
- What kind of legacy do you want to build for your children and grandchildren?

Because here's the truth:

This next chapter isn't about fading away. It's about rising up.

The world doesn't need more quiet retirees. It needs battle-tested men and women who are willing to step into a new mission—with purpose and power.

Because purpose doesn't retire. It just changes uniform.

PART II
The Shift Begins—
The Entrepreneur's Beat

CHAPTER FIVE

Picking Your Mission

*Choosing a business idea that aligns
with your skills, values, and passions.*

In the field, on the streets, or on the battlefield, the mission was handed to you.

A warrant. A patrol zone. A tactical operation. The objectives were clear. The rules were set. Most of time those missions, plans, operations, were set by somebody else.

Now? The mission is yours to define. No chain of command. No briefing room. No squad or team. Just you and the wide-open and unlimited opportunity to build something from the ground up.

This is where many retired or transitioning warriors get stuck.

They know they want more. They feel the fire. But they don't know where to aim it. They don't know what the first steps are to go down that path. It can be overwhelming, and that can be like quicksand.

The great and inspiring motivational speaker Les Brown talks about the graveyard. He said, *"The graveyard is the richest place on earth, because it is here that you will find all the hopes and dreams that were never fulfilled, the books that were never written, the songs that were never sung, the inventions that were never shared, the cures that were never discovered, all because someone was too afraid to take that first step, keep with the problem, or determined to carry out their dream."*

What a truthful yet sobering observation. I have often said, "The graveyard is full of unrealized million-dollar ideas, and a bunch of those died with a police officer or soldier." Those ideas died right along with whoever was too comfortable, too unsure, too susceptible to the critics, or too scared to bring those God-inspired ideas to life. Don't be selfish. Don't be scared. Don't take your million-dollar or potentially world-changing ideas to the grave with you.

This chapter is about finding your next mission—one built on your experience, fueled by your passion, and aligned with your purpose.

Start with What You Know

You've seen a lot. Learned a lot. Developed skills most people only dream of.

So ask yourself:

- What do I already know how to do better than most?
- What problems have I solved in my career that others still struggle with?
- What could I teach someone else that would change their life?

That's your advantage. That's your business foundation.

The power of "been there, done that."

I knew, even before I left the law enforcement career, that I wanted to be in business for myself. I had to ask myself these questions as well. I knew I was good at public speaking, so I set goals and made a plan to find more opportunities to speak about the things I'm passionate about, like law enforcement, leadership, and freedom. Most people are afraid to stand in front of a large group of people and share their expertise and passions, so I knew I had an advantage.

I also knew I wanted to start a consulting business. Being sheriff for eight years, combined with opportunities like *Live PD*, *60 Days In*, countless national media hits, and a successful social media presence, meant I was able to connect with hundreds of sheriffs, police chiefs, and other professionals in our fields. This would give me the ability to approach organizations and businesses in the law enforcement, border security, immigration, and mental health spaces, with the tools to help solve their problems in the marketplace. I knew those contacts and relationships that I had been able to forge through the years would be of value to those businesses and organizations.

I also had a desire to help my brothers and sisters in law enforcement and military put their skills, talents, and wisdom to good use and benefit them and their families. To build something. To find purpose and to act on it.

There's a reason military and law enforcement veterans make great entrepreneurs: We solve problems under pressure.

If you've led a unit, you can lead a team. If you've managed critical incidents, you can manage business operations. If you've taught recruits or trained new hires, you can create a course or coaching program.

The marketplace values real experience. And you've got it.

A Story: The Mission I Didn't Expect

I have loved being in law enforcement. I loved being the elected sheriff. I could've probably continued as sheriff for as long as I wanted to. Purpose was calling my name though. As much as I tried to ignore the promptings, I was feeling compelled to take on another challenge. I really thought that new chapter would be in the private sector, consulting and owning my own businesses. God had other plans.

In April of 2023, my wife and I decided, after much prayer and consideration, to enter the race for US Senate for Arizona. I know, what the hell were we thinking? We thought we were crazy too, and we probably were. We felt that purpose in our hearts. We weren't sure whether we would win or not, but we knew we needed to take on the mission.

We spent 2023 and most of 2024 running all over the state, grinding away day in and day out. I was still the sheriff and spent at least forty hours a week doing that job, and I ran for Senate all across the state of Arizona. While it was challenging to say the least, we also found it to be masochistically fulfilling and rewarding. We knew, win or lose, we were again adding tools to our toolbox that hardly anybody would be able to say they had. We had no doubt those newly acquired skills and the more honed-in possessed skills would make me even more valuable in the marketplace.

I could write a separate book on the Senate run, but let me just give you the cliff notes: I lost. I ran the race I wanted to run, but it wasn't enough. Victory was not in the cards.

In running for Senate, I wasn't able to run for two elected offices simultaneously, so I couldn't run for sheriff. That meant, win or lose in the Senate race, my time as sheriff would be over on December 31, 2024.

After I had lost my bid for the US Senate in the primary election, everybody asked me, "What are you going to do now, Sheriff?" They asked as if all I knew was law enforcement, as if my identity and purpose were tied to being the sheriff. Little did they know I already had a plan. I was ready for the next mission. That mission? Entrepreneurship.

After I officially stepped down as sheriff, I thought I'd focus on family, write another book, do some more public speaking, and start my consulting company and a couple other businesses. However, just as I expected, everywhere I went, I kept hearing the same thing from veterans and former LEOs when we talked about entrepreneurship:

"If I retire, what will I do?"

"I don't know anything about starting a business."

"I don't know how to start."

"I want to do something more, but I'm not sure what."

"I feel like I still have fight in me, but I don't know where to put it."

That's when **Ten 7** really started forming in my mind—not just as videos or courses but as a mission.

What if I created a community to help men and women like us build their next chapter? What if we taught entrepreneurship in a way only we could understand—clear, straight, and backed by grit?

That became the mission.

At **Ten 7**, our mission is to empower retired law enforcement officers, first responders, veterans, and anyone seeking a new path to success by providing the tools, knowledge, and community support necessary to transition from public service to entrepreneurship. We believe that a career in law enforcement equips individuals with unique skills, leadership, and discipline that can serve as a strong foundation for building a thriving business.

And now you're reading this book because I said yes to it.

You Don't Need a Shark Tank Idea

Although if you had a Shark Tank idea, **Ten 7** would love to help you make that a reality.

Let's get one thing straight: You don't need a flashy app or a million-dollar startup idea to build your next chapter.

Some of the best businesses are simple:

- A mobile detailing company run by a Marine.
- A firearms safety course taught by a retired female detective.
- A beef jerky brand run by a deputy who makes the perfect jerky.
- A consulting business for law enforcement procurement.
- A Subway, a Five Guys, or a Chick-fil-A franchise.
- A handyman service, a podcast, a security training school.

Simple. Smart. Profitable. Purpose-driven.

Your mission doesn't have to be loud. It just has to be yours.

Choosing What Feeds Your Purpose

Too many people choose business ideas that look good on paper but leave them feeling drained. That's not what we're building here. You've spent a lifetime serving others, often sacrificing your own peace for the sake of the mission.

This next mission should energize you, not empty you.

When choosing what business or path to take on, ask yourself this: Does it give me energy, or does it take it away? Would I wake up excited to do this every day, even if the money doesn't show up right away? That kind of clarity matters.

This isn't about chasing the dollar. It's about choosing a mission that you can commit to with the same fire you brought to your service career.

Honor Your Season

One of the most powerful things about stepping into Ten 7 is that you get to work *with* your life, not against it.

If you're newly retired, you might want more freedom and less stress. That's okay.

You can build something small and scalable: a seasonal side hustle, a consultancy that takes one client a month, or a teaching role in your area of expertise.

If you're full of fire and want to go all-in, then build something bold. Just know that both paths are honorable. Ten 7 doesn't mean replicating your old sixty-hour workweeks. It means doing work on your terms, with your vision and values leading the way.

Build with the End in Mind

When you build your business, think legacy.

Is this something you could one day pass on to your kids? Could it fund your grandkids' education or be used to hire and mentor other veterans? Could it create jobs in your hometown or be something that changes the narrative around retirement?

Your next mission isn't just about replacing income, it's about replacing impact.

Don't think small. Think service. Think strategy. Think generational.

You've already spent your career building someone else's vision. Now it's your turn.

And just like your first mission, your next one will take planning, discipline, grit, and faith. The good news is you've got all that already.

Now it's time to aim it.

Checkpoint: Mission Discovery Exercise

Get out your notebook or use the worksheet in your Ten 7 membership. Write down:

Your skills: What are five things you're really good at (from your career, hobbies, or side jobs)?

Your passion: What fires you up? What topic could you talk about all day?

Your experience: What life experiences have taught you things most people wouldn't know?

Your vision: If you could solve one problem in your community, your industry, or your world, what would it be?

Now draw a circle where all four of those areas overlap. That's your mission. That's your business.

This isn't just the next step. It's the start of the mission you were always meant to lead.

CHAPTER SIX

Building Your Squad

Networking, mentorship, and community.
You were never meant to fight alone.

In the military, you had a unit. In law enforcement, you had a shift, a squad, dispatch, a backup channel. Even when you were working solo, you weren't ever truly alone.

You had someone to call. Someone to cover your six. Someone to lean on when the situation went sideways.

But when you step out of uniform, that radio goes quiet. And if you're not careful, so do you.

The strangest feeling about being retired is being alone. I had spent a career working with a team. As a sheriff I had chiefs, captains, lieutenants, assistants. I was used to having a lot of people whom I could call on to help carry out my vision, my mission. Team members who would help me execute my plans. Then, overnight, it was radio silence. No more assistant, no chiefs, no captains, no team. This feeling of being alone was going to take some getting used to.

The Dangerous Lie of the Lone Wolf

Somewhere along the line, we're taught to muscle through on our own. "I've got this." "I don't need help." "I'll figure it out."

That kind of thinking might keep you alive in a gunfight, but it'll kill your growth in business. You need a squad. You need a team.

Not just employees or partners, but real relationships. People who sharpen you. People who've been where you want to go. People who challenge you, support you, and keep you accountable.

I knew I was going to need a new team in this new chapter of life. I immediately enlisted my biggest lifelong supporter and teammate: my wife. She has been my biggest supporter, my most enthusiastic cheerleader, my most trusted confidant and my greatest asset.

Most startup businesses can't afford to hire or pay employees. Spouses or partners can be a viable option. They have a vested interest in making sure your dreams and passions become a reality. They benefit from a successful venture.

The flip side is that some spouses and significant others are risk averse. The idea of starting a new business or building something scares them. Sometimes they are not supportive. That's okay, it may take time for them to see your vision, to feel your passion, or to understand the mission. You will want them on your team eventually, so be patient.

I also saw an opportunity to enlist my adult kids. An opportunity to mentor them in business as well. The benefit of working with my children was I trusted them. Unlike new employees, I know their strengths and weaknesses. My children also understand the value of building a family business/operation, because they will ultimately be the heirs and benefactors of whatever we build. Children can be good team members.

Beware of taking on business partners. While the draw to create or be part of a team will push you toward taking on a business partner, think twice before you do it. Even if you share the same passion and mission, you are not the same. Your leadership styles may be different, your ideas of how to execute the mission may be different, your goals may be different. Building a business can be stressful as well, which can put a strain on even the best of friendships or brotherhoods. Success is even more threatening to a business partnership. Money and success can sour even the closest of relationships, and partnerships rarely come out unscathed or survive success. Think long and hard about entering into a partnership, no matter how enticing the "team" idea may be.

I have made this mistake...multiple times. I have learned the hard way that partnerships are difficult and often end poorly.

Avoid partnerships with family as well. I realize this sounds contradictory to what I just told you about hiring my adult children and working with my wife. That's different. My wife is not an official business partner and my children are my employees. They have growth potential, they will serve as board members and even have future ownership, but for now they are employees. Family members, especially outside your immediate family members, are very difficult. And unlike a business partnership with a friend or colleague where you can just walk away or sever the friendship, you have a blood relationship with family members. You will see them at family get-togethers, on holidays, at weddings, birthday parties, etc. It will be tough to avoid them after a bad partnership or business gone south. I highly recommend you resist the temptation of entering a business partnership with a family member.

Be the boss. Build your business. Create your empire. Go out, work hard, grind away, and use the success of your labors to build a great team.

The 3 Types of People Every Entrepreneur Needs

Mentors. Someone who's ahead of you on the road and willing to turn around and show you the way. They've made mistakes, built businesses, survived the stuff you're just now stepping into.

The bold, outspoken billionaire Dan Peña says, "Show me your friends and I will show you your future." Who we choose to surround ourselves with really does play a major role in our future and what kind of success we can expect. This is especially true in business.

Look for mentors. People who are doing better than you. Find people who have made the mistakes and figured out successful solutions. If you want to make more money, surround yourself with friends or mentors making more money than you. That will raise your game. Learn from them. Be a sponge. And when you surpass them, find another group of people who are making more than you.

If you want to be smarter, hang around people smarter than you.

If you want to learn more about marketing, surround yourself with people who are successful at marketing.

If you want to be successful as an entrepreneur, spend as much time as you can with other successful business owners.

You might be asking yourself, "So how do I find or meet those people?"

This is why I started Ten 7. We all need mentors. Ten 7 will give you the base, knowledge, and mentorship to build a great business. Once you have done that, we hope to see you become one of the valuable mentors to other people you will meet along the way, and pay it forward.

I have been fortunate along my journey over these last several years to mentor some people in my circle, just as others have helped me. Because I had written two books during my time as sheriff, I was able to mentor my chief deputy through setting up a business and writing his book about his amazing experiences over the years as a deputy. He has found great success with his perspective and his book has done very well.

Another example is a guy you may have heard of, Frank Sloup of *Fridays with Frank*. When we launched Fridays with Frank we never could have predicted the amount of success we had, for both our agency and for Frank personally. It all began as a public service video for a new texting and driving law that had passed in Arizona, but it caught on like wildfire. It became a weekly PSA, and then eventually turned into his own business and brand. Every week it grew and grew in popularity. As it grew in success I sat down with Frank and strongly encouraged him to take this new brand to the next level. I gave him my blessing within the agency to start selling merch and ramp up his business. That's what the entrepreneurial spirit can do when you have a growth mindset and apply business principles to things you may be doing already.

Allies. Fellow entrepreneurs or professionals on the same level as you. These are your sounding boards. The ones who "get it." They're fighting the same battles in different lanes. In war, you need good allies and alliances.

Sun Tzu taught that no warrior wins alone. Victory often hinges on the strength of your alliances. The same principle applies in business. Strategic partnerships—with other entrepreneurs, service providers, or industry experts—can open doors you couldn't kick down alone. These relationships bring fresh insight, access to new markets, and critical backup when challenges arise. In your former career, you relied on backup when the stakes were high. In business, your allies are your reinforcements— build those relationships with purpose.

Just as Sun Tzu emphasized the power of a disciplined and loyal army, your team in business matters more than any single strategy. Whether it's family or hired staff, your people are your front line. Foster a culture built on trust, clear communication, and mutual respect. Invest in their development. Empower them with purpose. You once led squads through chaos—now lead a business team with that same resolve and integrity.

Finally, Sun Tzu believed in aligning every move with clear, unified objectives. In your business, that means setting a mission that everyone—from family members to employees—can stand behind. Be transparent about your vision. Make sure your values aren't just words on a wall but lived out in daily decisions. When your team believes in the "why," they'll fight for the "how."

Apprentices. People you'll help, guide, or lead. When you teach others, you sharpen your own skills—and you multiply your impact.

Apprentices and interns can be excellent options to help you in your business, especially when you are getting started and have limited resources. This also gives you a chance to return the mentorship that you have received from others. Just as you sought more knowledge and skills, there are others looking to apprentice under your mentorship.

While you may be seeking to be mentored by more seasoned law enforcement, don't forget you possess a set of skills and experiences that others will never obtain.

Allowing for apprentices to come in and learn from you will keep you sharp and focused.

Bottom line, your mission is too important to do alone.

A Story: The Brotherhood Doesn't End— It Just Evolves

A few months after I stepped down as sheriff, I attended a summit where I was among a bunch of retired police chiefs from some of the biggest cities in this country. All men and women who had led hundreds, if not thousands of troops. Now, we were all consultants or advisors. No uniforms. No ranks. No titles.

Just stories, scars, and experience.

While we stood there talking about the profession, the changes, the things we didn't like and the things we missed, we eventually landed on the topic of business. Remember, this group was among the most accomplished in our profession, holding leadership positions in some of the largest and most influential law enforcement agencies.

I realized that as talented as many of them were, there was either a lack of or, at best, only basic knowledge of business structures and operations. I could see many of them in this group didn't truly grasp the opportunities that were in front of them. Their leadership, their knowledge, their wealth of contacts—they had everything they needed to be building very successful consulting businesses. Maybe they were comfortable with just one client. Maybe they were scared of their potential. Maybe their goals were too low.

I started to realize that even these guys from the highest levels of our profession now found themselves in a new playing field. No more chiefs, no more sheriffs, just business owners. They were on their own.

I also realized even the guys at the top had a lot to learn about entrepreneurship, branding, marketing, and business operations. They were basically rookies again.

That stuck with me, because so many of us feel like rookies when we take off the badge; in reality, we're seasoned operators stepping into a new arena.

That day continued to help me shape Ten 7. That moment of conversation became a network. That network became momentum.

And that's how missions grow.

Where to Find Your Squad

You don't need to wait for the perfect networking event or a formal invitation.

Start simple:

- Tap into veteran-owned business groups.
- Join Ten 7's member community.
- Reach out to someone you admire and ask for fifteen minutes of advice.
- Attend an entrepreneur meetup or business training.
- Host a coffee with three like-minded leaders and share goals.
- Listen to good podcasts, like the *Ten 7 Podcast*, or other motivating and educational videos.

And just like on patrol, always know who's riding with you. Not everyone deserves to be in your car.

Squad Roles: Beyond Friendship

Your squad isn't just your buddies. It's a strategic asset. You want people who serve specific roles in your growth.

You need people who will support you and cheer you on. Sometimes those closest to us, whether it be family or friends, are the worst dream killers. Maybe it's out of jealousy, maybe it's out of fear and wanting to protect you, maybe it's because they don't want to lose you to the business, or maybe they just don't realize they are being negative. Whatever their reasoning, don't let them kill your dreams, your ideas, or your passion.

While you want to steer clear of the negative and doubtful voices, you still need someone to call you out when you're drifting. Someone who challenges your business ideas with hard truth. Someone who has been in the fight longer—and survived.

That doesn't mean you cut ties with old friends, but it does mean you get intentional about who gets access to your time and your energy in this next season.

Friendship is great. Brotherhood is sacred. But mission-driven relationships are where you find traction.

Traits of a Solid Squad Member

Here's what to look for when building your squad:

- **Loyalty.** You've had your back watched. You know what loyalty feels like. In business, you need people who will tell the truth *and* show up when it matters.
- **Respect.** Not just mutual respect, but someone who respects the mission you're building, even if it's not theirs.
- **No Ego.** There's no room for ego in the debrief or in the war room. You need people secure enough to admit when they're wrong and wise enough to help when you are.
- **Follow-Through.** Talk is cheap. Squad members show up, follow through, and stay engaged when things get tough.

Remember, your next mission might be personal, but it's never private. You'll need a team.

The Danger of Isolation

One of the top contributors to depression and failed ventures among veterans and first responders is isolation.

When we step out of uniform, we lose structure. We lose connection. And if we're not careful, we retreat into our own heads.

But you know this: "Nothing good happens when backup doesn't show up."

This chapter is a reminder: Don't go dark.

Let people in. Reach out. Share your wins and your struggles.

You weren't built to battle alone.

Your final Ten 7 doesn't mean you're off duty. It means you're on a new team. And now you get to build that team with purpose.

Checkpoint: Squad Assessment

Answer these questions:

- Who in my life has the experience I want to learn from? Have I reached out to them?

- Do I have a go-to circle of allies who understand the grind of building something?
- Who's one person I could mentor or support through their own transition?
- Is there anyone on my team who drains me more than drives me? Am I willing to fix that?

Iron sharpens iron. You've always been stronger with the right team behind you.

Now it's time to build your next squad—the one that helps you win the next battle.

CHAPTER SEVEN

Risk and Reward

Law enforcement and military folks understand risk.
Now it's about learning how to manage
and leverage it in the business world.

If you've worn the badge or the uniform, you've already lived with risk. Every traffic stop. Every knock on a door. Every time you strapped on your vest or walked into the unknown, you didn't run from risk. You ran toward it.

But here's the difference: In service, the risk was assigned. In business, the risk is chosen. And that's what makes it scary.

Over the last couple of decades I have worked with some really courageous people who pushed past any fear and ran into or toward the most dangerous of situations. I've seen police officers pursue a vehicle at high speeds, occupied by armed suspects who were just involved in a shooting, without hesitation. I've seen police and firefighters run into a burning building, without a second thought for the own lives, to save a child or even a pet. I've heard stories of combat soldiers in a far-off land, busting through doors of unknown buildings to stop armed terrorists. That is risk.

However, those same police and military soldiers, as unafraid and brave as they have proven to be, can be stopped dead in their tracks with the thought and fear of change or starting a new business.

Change can be scary for us. Maybe it's because we haven't trained for the risks that starting a new business or making a major life change would bring. Through training and experience, we actually have learned to manage these risks as well.

Entrepreneurship is a Risk Game

Starting a business means betting on yourself. It means stepping out on your own, without backup. It means knowing there's no steady paycheck, no pension, no guaranteed outcome.

And for some, that feels reckless. But for warriors like us? That feels familiar, because we know how to manage risk. We've done it our entire careers.

In fact, we've been conditioned for it. From our early days on the force or in the military, we were trained to see threats, anticipate danger, and still move forward. That kind of courage doesn't disappear—it evolves.

So let's talk about what that evolution looks like.

A Story:
The Night That Could've Cost Me Everything

It was a dark and quiet night on the reservation where I worked as a gang and drug detective. Our job as the gang and drug unit was to disrupt and dismantle gang and drug activity, and we were good at doing just that. We spent so much time going after the gang bangers that we often found ourselves too desensitized to the things that that should have made us fearful.

I was driving alone in my unmarked patrol past one of the gang houses where we commonly had calls for service. As I slowly drove by the house, I could see two of the known gang bangers standing in the driveway, leaning against the trunk of the vehicle. Being that I was in a white unmarked Ford Explorer, I don't think they realized who I was. Or maybe they did.

Just as I passed the residence, I heard the familiar sound—*crack, crack*—of gunshots piercing the still of the night. I immediately flipped around and turned off my headlights. As I pulled up behind a big tree, which was blocking the view of the street, I heard it again—*crack, crack*. This time it was even louder. I didn't know if they were shooting at me or not, but it didn't matter. I was going in.

I gassed it for the last forty feet, quickly slamming my brakes to a stop. The two men bolted toward the carport. I jumped out of my vehicle and was in foot pursuit of the armed suspects. They ran through the dimly lit carport and out into a pitch-black field behind the residence. I was sprinting after them at full speed. When I got to the rear of the carport, ready to run out after them into the pitch black, I heard something inside me say, "STOP!" This wasn't like me. I wasn't scared, but I had learned to trust my gut. I realized I was backlit by the lights of the carport, putting me at a dangerous tactical disadvantage. I listened to my gut.

Up to that point I had been taking the risk, no fear, chasing after two armed gang bangers by myself. My gut and acquired instinct said, "The *risk* is not worth the *reward*."

While I would have been at a tactical disadvantage had I continued, I decided to adjust and take the advantage. I called out my team. We methodically and tactically searched the area and the field. We eventually found the two suspects in the residence, covered in fresh mud, lying on the bed of the primary bedroom pretending to be asleep. Once we had them in custody and the scene was secure, I went back out to the field and within ten minutes found two handguns.

That could have gone very differently. It could have been the end for me. I was willing to take the risk until I wasn't. In this job I learned to trust my training, my instincts, and God...and I'm pretty sure God stepped in that night.

I'll never forget that foot chase and then the distinct impression to stop. Why do we take on those risks? Because that's what we do. We read the situation, make the best call, and move forward anyway. That's *risk management*.

Now, in business, I use that same gut instinct. Whether I'm deciding on a deal, launching a product, or choosing an employee, I remember that night. I remember what it felt like to step forward in spite of the fear.

A Story: Pigeon Crap and Rooftop Risks

Before I became a cop, I owned a pigeon control business. Not exactly glamorous, but somebody had to do it. The job consisted of climbing up on roofs, dealing with filth, fighting gravity and guano—every day was a risk.

At six feet, three inches and 240 pounds, I wasn't built for balancing on roof tiles. I nearly fell more than once. The work was hard, gross, and honestly dangerous.

I did it anyway.

Why? Because I had mouths to feed. And over time, I got better. The risk didn't go away, but I learned how to manage it. I placed ladders better. I moved slower. I scanned every step. I kept climbing the ladder—literally and figuratively.

That same mindset helped me when I transitioned into law enforcement. My wife used to say she worried *less* about me as a cop than she did when I was cleaning pigeon nests.

That's risk perspective. And in business, you'll need that perspective too.

Risk Is in My DNA

I was raised by a man who taught me not just how to live, but how to take a chance on something bigger than myself. My dad never worked for anyone. He was an entrepreneur through and through. I watched him build businesses in places like Hawaii, the Philippines, and Panama.

He never once discouraged me from taking risks. In fact, he expected it. That upbringing taught me that risk was part of life—not something to fear, but something to respect. My mom was more cautious, but she was strong enough to support my dad through every high and low.

That upbringing shaped me. I didn't grow up thinking I'd be a cop or a sheriff. I started businesses. I failed in some. I succeeded in others. And each time I took a hit, I dusted off and went again.

That's what risk teaches you: **resilience**. That's what business demands: **faith in your own fire**.

Understanding the Types of Risk: Calculated vs. Emotional Risk

In business, not all risks are equal. Here's how I see it:

- **Calculated Risk:** You've done your homework. You know the downside. But the potential upside is worth it. This is how businesses grow.
- **Emotional Risk:** You're operating from pride or panic. That's dangerous. We've all seen it on the streets—bad calls made in the heat of the moment. Don't bring that into your business.
- **Growth Risk:** It stretches you. It scares you. But deep down, you know it's the next step. That's the edge where life changes.

You don't have to eliminate risk. You just have to respect it. Manage it. Use it.

Courage Is a Muscle

One of the greatest lies we've been told is that courage is the absence of fear. It's not.

Courage is fear—under control. The very definition of courage is "not deterred by danger or pain." It doesn't insinuate there won't be any fear or danger or pain. Courage is what it takes to do it anyway, despite all of that. It's action in the face of the unknown. It's stepping forward regardless of the danger and pain.

And courage, like any muscle, gets stronger the more you use it.

From the Streets to the Campaign Trail

When I decided to run for sheriff, I took one of the biggest risks of my life. I started my campaign in 2015. As I wrote in my book, *American Sheriff: Rules to Live By*, "I didn't have the money. I didn't have the connections. But I had a confirmation in my soul that I needed to do it. I wasn't even sure what the reward would look like—I just knew I had to see what was behind the curtain."

I was the underdog: one-quarter of the funding, one-third of the experience, and little to no name recognition. But I believed in what I stood for. And I believed bold risks were rewarded.

I gave up income. I started three businesses just to make the extra money I would need for the campaign. I traded family time, security, and comfort for a shot at a mission I believed in. I took the leap. I took the risk. And with hard work, divine guidance, and the support of good people—I won.

And the rewards? They weren't just about the title. They were about proving something to myself: I could lead, take the hits, and stay true. That I could risk it all and still sleep well at night.

And you know what? That wasn't the last big risk I took.

Leading up to my second term as sheriff, the country was in turmoil. A few very public events involving police led to major backlash against law enforcement across the country. There was a huge movement to defund police, which was a ridiculous idea. Tremendous pressure was put on law enforcement and agencies to bend the knee. We did not. We stood tall.

All that was compounded by COVID. Media and politicians fueled the fears of Americans all across the country and globe. To take a stand against it would be risky, right?

Anybody can do what's right when it's easy and the norm. Can you stand up for freedom, the Constitution, and what's right when the entire world is against you?

I took a very public stand against lockdowns, mandates, and media pressure during COVID—that was another high-stakes decision. I risked public opinion, political capital, and my career. But I stood firm. Because if we won't risk for what's right, what are we doing here?

And I won.

Not just the election, but the respect of a community that saw I was willing to lead from the front, no matter the cost, no matter the risk.

And that's a principle I still carry today.

Fear of the Unknown

The truth is, most of our fears are like my fear of snakes. I've never been bitten. I've never been chased by one. But my imagination has done a number on me.

That's how most fear works. We fear what we *don't* know, what we *imagine.*

People fear clowns, zombies, failure. None of them are real threats in the daily grind, but they live large in the mind. In business, the unknown feels like a snake pit. But more often than not, there are no snakes—just shadows.

That's why boldness matters. Because most of the time, we're fighting imaginary enemies. We are too worried or focused on what will likely never be.

Fear Is Not the Enemy

Fear is a signal. A tool. The same instincts that kept you alive on patrol can guide you in business. But here's the catch: **Fear isn't a stop sign. It's a green light with caution.**

You can feel fear and still move forward. That's courage. You can weigh the cost and still take the shot. That's leadership. And you can do it when everyone around you thinks you're crazy. That's entrepreneurship.

A Story: The Golf Course and the Vaccine Mandate

I remember playing a round of golf with a friend. He'd taken the vaccine and asked why I hadn't. I laid it out in business terms: "I've got a 99 percent chance of not getting COVID. And if I do, I'll likely survive. Why would I take something unproven that might not work, when my odds are already good?"

That's what I call **risk versus reward**.

Then I made a video for my department saying we wouldn't be mandating the vaccine. It was a bold stance—one that brought backlash. But guess what? That video went viral. And the reward? Officers from across the country applied to work for us. Why? Because we took a risk to protect freedom and our people.

A Story from the Founders: Robert Morris

Robert Morris was one of the wealthiest men in early America. He didn't just sign the Declaration of Independence, he *funded* the war. He literally bet his fortune on the idea of freedom.

He lost it all. Died broke. But he changed history.

That's what real risk looks like. And that's why the quote from Kipling's poem "If—" rings so true: "If you can make one heap of all your winnings / And risk it on one turn of pitch-and-toss / And lose, and start again at your beginnings / And never breathe a word about your loss..."

Checkpoint: Know Your Risk Profile

Take a moment to answer these:

- What risks have I taken that changed my life?
- What am I holding back from because of fear?
- What's the worst thing that could happen if I take this next leap?
- What's the best thing that could happen if I don't?

Final Thought: Roulette and Reward

Life's a bit like a roulette table. You can play it safe—spread your chips everywhere and pray for a small win. Or you can put it all on one number and spin.

High risk. High reward.

You won't always win. But you'll always grow, and risk can be exhilarating! And more importantly, you'll live.

Like I always say, you can die choking on a potato chip sitting on your couch. May as well give life hell while you've got it.

Ten 7 isn't just a code for "end of watch." It's a signal that something has ended, and something else is about to begin. That moment of silence... That's the space where courage is reborn. Where you choose to take the risk. And step into who you were always meant to become.

Now it's time to face down the fear of building something for yourself. **Risk isn't the enemy. Fear isn't the enemy. Wasting your potential is.** You're not reckless. You're ready.

CHAPTER EIGHT

The Business Mindset

Rewiring the brain from reactive response to proactive planning. The discipline you mastered applies here—just differently.

In your previous life, you didn't have the luxury of waiting around.

The tones dropped. The radio cracked. The mission began.

You were trained to react. Trained to adapt. Trained to move fast and decisively.

But here's the catch: That same reactive mindset will burn you out in business.

In entrepreneurship, success comes to those who learn how to think ahead, plan strategically, and stay disciplined—without a commanding officer breathing down their neck.

You don't need to lose your edge. You just need to sharpen it differently.

From Reactive to Proactive

In the field, your calendar belonged to someone else. The next call, the next shift, the next incident, the next deployment—you followed orders. You adapted to chaos.

As first responders or military, you train for months, long before you even attempt to do the job. You spent hundreds of hours sweating, studying, working through training scenarios. That was being proactive. You were trained for the calls, for the battles, for the foot chases, for the vehicle pursuits, for the lifesaving moments, so that you would react the right way.

Just like on the streets or in combat zones, we can't control what circumstances we will need to react to, but we can be proactive in preparing to the best of our abilities so that we can react appropriately. The business world is the same. We proactively prepare by learning how to set up the right business, by creating a good business plan, by working up an effective marketing strategy, and by mastering our craft, so we can react appropriately when the circumstances present themselves. The other difference is, depending on what kind of business or idea or brand you decide to create, it will most likely not involve life or death situations. What a relief! Mistakes in business may cost you time and money, but they usually don't cost lives.

The other benefit is that now you own the clock. You own the plan. You own the results.

And that requires a new kind of mental toughness—one rooted in clarity, ownership, and consistency.

This will be a new feeling for most of you. You spent the majority of your career complaining about leadership. You talked about—and rightfully so in many cases—how those supervisors didn't belong in leadership positions. You questioned decisions. You especially hated change.

I have always quipped that police officers—and this probably goes for soldiers as well—hate two things: They hate the way things are and they hate change. So basically, they hate everything. Change just happens to be one of the most hated things.

You hate new policies. You hate changing equipment. You hate shift change. You hate your supervisors. You hate their replacements. I think you get the picture.

The truth is, the main reason you hated change was probably because you didn't have all of the information for the change. You were likely reactive to the change because you didn't understand all of the ins and outs of the decisions that were being made by your agency leadership. That is understandable. Nobody likes being in the dark without a flashlight. My experience as a leader is that a little bit of communication and involvement goes a long way to reducing the resistance and hate of change.

When you begin to hire employees for your business, let this serve as a reminder that if you want to reduce the negative reactions to changes you make, communicate.

A Story: The Mindset Shift

As I mentioned, before I became a police officer, I was a businessman. I had taken risks. I had successes. I had failures. I had to market my products. I had to put business plans together.

When I went through the academy at thirty-four years old, I was older than most of my fellow cadets. I had life experiences that most of them, especially the younger cadets, did not have. This was an advantage for me. I was self-motivated and understood sales. I could see the value of my business experience immediately. And when I graduated, this again set me apart from my fellow officers. I created a plan for success, trained for success, and executed it in the field.

I just had to make a *mindset shift*.

Years later, when I successfully won my bid for sheriff, I continued to see the value.

My command staff, consisting of my chief deputy, my deputy chief over the road, and my deputy chief over the jail, had no business experience. They had all been police officers/deputies since they were young. It was their first job and they had become masters of their crafts. They had put in the time, they had trained, and they were really effective law enforcement officials and leaders.

As the elected sheriff I wanted to bring a mindset shift. I wanted to implement more business principles into the way we ran the sheriff's office. This was new and uncomfortable for my command staff. I wanted to fix the disastrous budget we inherited by implementing a solid business plan to the board of supervisors. We put together a plan that would put us in a position to fix the budget within two years. This was unfamiliar territory for my chiefs. We needed that mindset shift. Even though we were government, and critics would say we couldn't run it like a business, we disagreed. We had investors: the taxpayers. We had a product we were selling: community safety, protecting constitutional rights, and law enforcement. We wanted to give our "investors" the best return on investment without going over budget.

While my command staff trusted me and understood that as sheriff I had the ultimate say-so, they were still nervous about the methods.

There wasn't just the budgeting. We also had to create a business plan for increasing employee morale, a business plan for marketing, a business plan for community engagement, a business plan for jail management and inmate recidivism. It was one giant business and my team members were quick learners. They learned to trust the plans and they learned to trust me.

Much of the trust, especially when it came to marketing the agency, came down to them learning to trust their gut in a different way than they were used to. Their gut instinct had kept them safe from harm, from bad situations, and allowed them to decipher between truth and lies. So understandably, whenever I would introduce a new or crazy marketing idea, their gut instinct to protect would kick in. They wanted to protect me, to protect the agency. Marketing was not something they knew or were trained for. This was the hardest mindset shift for them. They had to learn to trust their gut for the marketing or business risks we would take.

Marketing is very overlooked and underutilized in the law enforcement profession. Like my command staff, most chiefs and sheriffs are career lawmen. That's not always a bad thing, but over the years they become institutionalized to government operations. Risk reduction and situational control has been drilled into them from day one, so they have a tough time accepting or implementing new ideas or practices. That stagnation, institutionalization, fear of change or whatever the reason, is to the detriment of our profession. We have become stuck in what we know, and it has affected officer/deputy hiring and how the community perceives law enforcement. The good news is, all those things can be improved with a simple mindset shift.

As a sheriff, I couldn't understand why agencies, chiefs, and sheriffs weren't more engaged on social media and in business practices. Those agency heads were missing tremendous opportunities to bridge the gap between the community and law enforcement. They were failing to use social media as a tool to showcase their agencies to those who were interested in a career in our profession. Those leaders were letting the media and the critics set the narrative instead of taking control. I get that social media puts us out there, and that scares most heads of agencies. It can be risky to post about the work we do. It can be uncomfortable to take control of the narrative. However, those agency heads better shift their mindset.

Law enforcement needs leaders. Bold men and women who aren't afraid to take risks, to be truthful and open with the community, and to stand up for your people. Stop fighting change. Be creative. Treat it like a business.

That's the mindset shift.

Discipline is the New Deployment

Here's more good news: You already have the discipline. You've shown up for early shifts, stuck to training schedules, followed protocol, stayed sharp under stress. Now that discipline is your greatest business weapon.

Daily structure = momentum

Clear goals = direction

Consistent habits = results

When you're disciplined, you're like a sharpened, well-tempered sword. That allows you to go out and operate in the world.

Discipline is found in our daily routines and rituals. You may have used discipline on occasion, but you still may not be disciplined. There is a difference between having discipline and being disciplined. When you *have* discipline, you're selective. When you have discipline, you're conditional. When you *are* disciplined, it's who you are. You show up to everything at one thousand percent. When you are disciplined, everything you do is striving for excellence.

Be disciplined.

In business being disciplined will be the difference between success or failure. Staying disciplined to the business plan rather than how you feel. Staying disciplined to the marketing plan. Staying disciplined to the work that needs to be done. Make discipline who you *are*.

Set goals. Big goals.

To be successful in business you will need to set goals. This will give you the direction, the compass to stay on course. Building and running a business is not easy. There will be many days when you want to give up. You may question whether you are heading in the right direction. During those tough times, it will be your goals that will keep you pushing in the right direction.

We also set goals to push ourselves further than we thought we were capable of going. Our goals should scare us. If they don't scare you, your goals aren't big enough. Be realistic but bold. You will be surprised by what you can accomplish when you set those goals.

There is a great documentary called *14 Peaks: Nothing Is Impossible*. If you haven't seen this yet I highly recommend you watch prior to setting your business goals. The documentary is about a Nepali man named Nims Purja, who decided to set the impossible goal to climb fourteen peaks. Why fourteen peaks? There are only fourteen peaks or mountains in the world that are higher than 8,000 meters. The fastest time to climb all fourteen peaks was seven years. Nims was going to climb all fourteen peaks in seven months.

When people heard that some unknown guy had set the goal to climb all fourteen peaks in seven months, their first reaction was, "Who the hell is Nims Purja?" Their second reaction was, "That's impossible!"

Nobody thought Nims would succeed. As a matter of fact, everybody told Nims his goal was "impossible." He heard that phrase so much that he decided to call his endeavor "Project Possible."

I don't want to give away the whole documentary, but there were a couple parts that really hit me.

The first was peak number four, Mount Everest.

Mount Everest was crawling with hundreds of mountain climbers who set out to achieve their goal of climbing the highest mountain in the world. Many of the climbers had trained their entire lives to climb this mountain.

Nims's goal wasn't just to climb Mount Everest like the other climbers. No, his goal was much bigger. Nims set the goal to climb Mount Everest, Lhotse, and Makalu, the first, fourth, and fifth highest mountains in the world, and he was going to do it in forty-eight hours. Nobody had ever done that before.

While climbing Mount Everest, Nims and Team Project Possible overtook 95 percent of the climbers on the mountain. There was only a two-day window of weather to climb the mountain, so it was packed with over three hundred climbers. That did not stop them from achieving their unprecedented goal of climbing those three mountains in forty-eight hours.

The second and most impactful part of the documentary was peak number ten, K2, at 8,611 meters.

When they arrived at K2 they were met with some bad weather, including three avalanches. The weather had kept the seasoned climbers from climbing the mountain. Many of them had made multiple attempts, only to turn around because of the weather and fear. They were stressed and feeling the despair, and then along came Nims and Team Project Possible.

Nims and his team brought their confidence and unstoppable attitude. As they began to lay out the plan to the other climbers, the other climbers got angry with Nims. They were fearful and tried to tell Nims all the reasons why they couldn't do it. Nims and his team pushed on anyway.

Of course, Nims and his team were successful in climbing K2. After they climbed it, twenty-four of the climbers who had been unsuccessful prior to Nims and his team arriving also climbed K2. They just needed a fearless leader to break through, somebody they could follow.

What hit me the hardest was the size of the goals. All of the climbers on K2 had set a very impressive goal to climb that mountain, but only that mountain. Nims and his team had set out to climb fourteen peaks, so number ten was not going to stop him or his team. It couldn't stop them, or their goal of climbing fourteen peaks in seven months would have been in jeopardy. Their goal was too big for them to be stuck and unsuccessful on one mountain. What if the other hikers had set bigger goals? What if they had decided to climb two mountains? Would they have let themselves be so deterred by one mountain?

The difference was the size of the goals. The size of the goals increased the resolve, the confidence, the determination, and the grit of Nims and his team.

Set goals that scare you and other people. Project Possible.

You also need to read your goals every day. Memorize your goals. Make them part of your daily conversations. Make them so real that there won't be any way that you don't achieve them.

There is a poem that my wife loves to recite from the book, *Think and Grow Rich* by Napoleon Hill. "I bargained with Life for a penny, / And Life would pay no more, / However I begged at evening / When I counted my scanty store. / For Life is a just employer, / He gives you what you ask, / But once you have set the wages, / Why, you must bear the task. / I worked for a menial's hire, / Only to learn, dismayed, / That any wage I had asked of Life, / Life would have willingly paid."

The universe will give you what you ask for and what you are disciplined enough to go after.

The last few months as a sheriff, my closest friend asked me what my goal was for the next year. I had an idea of what I wanted to make on a monthly basis, but I hadn't committed it to paper. I hadn't made it a goal. That was the nudge I needed to get my goals set. I made a clear and conscious decision of what I wanted to make every month and I wrote it down. Then I decided what I wanted to make for the year, and I wrote it down. In January, the first full month after my official retirement, I was already hitting my monthly goal...and it was not a small number. It was ten times what my take-home was as a sheriff, but I had ingrained that goal so deeply into my everyday thinking that I never questioned whether it would happen.

Here is the crazy part: I hit the goal I set, which I thought was a big and bold goal, but that was it. It capped at what I had set in my mind. I realized then that I wasn't bold enough. I have since rewritten my monthly and yearly goals with even more boldness, and I am already seeing the results of those goals.

Don't bargain with life for a penny, because life would have paid more. All you have to do is ask. Set goals. Big goals.

Be consistent.

Consistent discipline and consistent good habits can't help but produce good results. Anybody can get up in the morning and say, "I think I will lose some weight," but only the disciplined and consistent ones will actually achieve the results. What are the results? Your goals.

I have had several businesses that didn't pan out, that's part of being an entrepreneur. Not every pan has gold. However, when I look back and take a full account of where I may have gone wrong, it usually led back to a lack of consistency.

One of the most important areas of consistency should be in sales and marketing. Equally important is consistent quality work or delivering your products and services in a consistent timely manner. However, without consistent sales and marketing, it won't matter how good your work is or how great your products and services are. You could be the most talented brick layer, but if nobody is out selling or marketing your product, nobody will know.

I have a friend who is one of the best salesmen I know. He has spent over three decades selling, and most of that has been door-to-door. He has been very successful, no matter what product he is selling. The reason why? Discipline, grit, and consistency. He knows that every day he has to be out there knocking on doors, selling, and marking his products. Rain, snow, sunny days, or whether he feels like working or not, he consistently puts in the sales and marketing work. Even if the sales aren't landing, he is still consistent. That consistency produces results for him and his business.

Be structured, be clear with your goals, be disciplined, and be consistent.

Mindset Matters More Than Strategy

You can have the best business plan in the world, but if your mind isn't right—if you don't believe in what you're doing or stay committed when it gets hard—it won't matter.

The most successful entrepreneurs aren't the smartest in the room, they're the ones who refuse to quit.

Strategic Thinking: Your New Weapon

In law enforcement or the military, you train for contingencies. In business, it's the same—only now, you're not just avoiding danger, you're identifying opportunity.

Strategic thinking means asking yourself daily:

- Where am I going?
- What resources do I need?
- What roadblocks might I face, and how will I address them?

This kind of thinking doesn't come naturally to everyone. But for you? It's second nature. You've done it for years. You just need to apply it to this new battlefield. You're not reacting anymore. You're designing.

The Cost of Complacency

One of the hidden dangers in entrepreneurship is comfort.

After years of high-stakes environments, business might seem slow, even boring. However, here's the warning: Complacency kills businesses the same way it kills operational readiness.

If you stop growing, stop evaluating, stop pushing—you'll stall. The mission will falter.

Just like you trained, qualified, and reviewed tactics, your business needs ongoing calibration.

- Review your numbers weekly.
- Evaluate your strengths and weaknesses monthly.
- Adjust your strategy quarterly.

Stay sharp. Stay engaged. Stay dangerous—in the best way.

Own the Mission

When you were in the field, you didn't get to pick the call. Now you do.

This is your business. Your brand. Your name on the door. That means your results are no one else's responsibility. No more blaming the chain of command. No more waiting on orders. Every win—and every loss—is yours to own.

That's not a burden. That's freedom. Because when you own the mission—you also own the victory.

And if you bring the same intensity, honor, and preparation to your business that you brought to the badge? There's nothing you can't build.

Checkpoint: Business Mentality Bootcamp

Take a few minutes to answer:

- What time do I wake up each day, and is it setting the tone for success?
- Do I have a clear daily routine that moves me closer to my business goals?

- Am I spending more time reacting to problems—or preparing to prevent them?
- When things get tough, do I have a mindset that says, "Adapt and overcome"?

You've already learned to lead in chaos. Now it's time to lead with clarity.

The same mindset that helped you survive the streets, the base, or the battlefield is the same mindset that will help you dominate in business.

Discipline. Preparation. Ownership. That's the real tactical advantage.

CHAPTER NINE

The Entrepreneur's Toolkit

Incorporating lessons on banking, business structure, legal protections, and tax readiness. These connect to Ten 7's online video modules and worksheets.

You wouldn't head out on patrol without your vest, your weapon, or your radio.

Same goes for business.

Too many good men and women step into entrepreneurship with passion and purpose, but no plan, no structure, and no systems.

The result? Burnout. Confusion. Missed opportunity.

That ends here.

This chapter and **Ten 7** give you the basic tools every new entrepreneur needs to operate smart, stay legal, and grow something real.

Tool 1: Your Business Structure

Before you make a dime, you need to decide how your business will be set up. What does that mean? What type of business structure will you choose?

One of the reasons I decided to write this book and start the Ten 7 membership website was because for years I have worked around first responders and military who had limited to no knowledge about business. When I would talk to fellow cops or veterans about my different business ventures or ideas, they would say, "How do you know what to do? I wouldn't know the first thing about how to start a business."

Those conversations are what started to plant the seed of Ten 7 in my head. We would create a community where our warriors could learn about starting a business and find that support community of fellow law enforcement and veterans who were mutually invested in each other's success.

While **Ten 7** has a lot to teach you, let's start with the basics of business structure.

Here are the basics:

Sole Proprietorship
Simple. Low cost. But you carry all liability personally.

For more information on what a sole proprietorship is and how to set it up, check out the full video at *https://goten7.com*.

LLC (Limited Liability Company)

Most common for small businesses. Protects your personal assets. Offers flexibility in how you're taxed.

For more information on what an LLC (Limited Liability Company) is and how to set it up, check out the full video at https://goten7.com.

S Corporation / C Corporation

More complex. Comes with tax advantages if you're growing or bringing on investors.

For more information on what S Corporations and C Corporations are and how to set them up, check out the full video at https://goten7.com.

Recommendation: Start with an LLC—easy to set up, protects your family, and gives you room to grow. Your membership with **Ten 7**, which you can sign up for at https://goten7.com, includes the setup of an LLC. Let us at **Ten 7** help get you going on the right path to business success.

Tool 2: Your EIN (Employer Identification Number)

This is your business's social security number. With the exception of a Sole Proprietorship, you'll need an EIN to open a bank account, pay taxes, and hire anyone.

- Free to get from the IRS
- Apply online in under ten minutes
- You'll use it for almost every business form

As part of your **Ten 7** membership, we would love to help you get your EIN and learn how to use it. Please reach out to one of our **Ten 7** team members or somebody from our legal team.

Tool 3: Your Bank and Budget

Rule #1: Don't mix personal and business money.

- Open a separate business checking account
- Track every expense and income from day one
- Use software like QuickBooks, Wave, or FreshBooks

Tip: Treat your business account like a squad car—you don't let just anyone ride in it. Keep it clean and documented.

For more information about banking and budgeting for your business, please join the **Ten 7** *community at* *https://goten7.com for complete videos from our experts. Our team can help you with your banking and budgeting questions.*

Tool 4: Your Basic Systems

Every business—whether you're selling T-shirts or tactical training—needs a few simple systems:

- *Customer Contact List.* Use a spreadsheet or CRM (Customer Relations Management system). Track who you talk to, what they need, and when to follow up.
- *Invoicing System.* You can use services like Square, Stripe, or PayPal to bill and accept payments.
- *Online Presence.* At minimum:
  - A professional email address (not Gmail)
  - A one-page website or landing page
  - A social media profile to establish trust

Remember: If people can't find you, they can't pay you.

*For more information about CRM (Customer Relations Management) tools, setting up and establishing an online presence, professional emails, or social media for your business, please join the **Ten 7** community at https://goten7.com for complete videos from our experts. Our team can help you with your CRM, website, email, and social media questions.*

A Story: A Near Miss on a $10,000 Mistake

A friend of mine, a retired detective, started a self-defense training business. Great course, loyal clients, doing everything right—except one thing: he hadn't officially formed his business. His structure wasn't properly set up and he didn't have business insurance.

One day, during a class, a participant slipped and twisted their ankle. They sued.

Due to the fact that he had no LLC in place, the lawsuit hit him personally. Instead of the liability being siloed in the LLC, it fell on his personal shoulders and he was personally liable. His house, his savings—all exposed.

A simple Limited Liability Company legal structure could've shielded him and his family. The right business structure would have contained the liability, and the business insurance would have stepped in to settle the claim against the business.

He's fine now—got it all straightened out—but it was a costly lesson. And it's one I hope you avoid.

Do it right!

*Your membership with **Ten 7**, which you can sign up for at https://goten7.com, includes the setup of an LLC. Let us* at **Ten 7** protect your business as well as you and your family from liability.

Tool 5: Your Advisors

Even in business, you need backup.

At minimum, find:

- A small business attorney (for contracts and legal advice)
- A CPA or tax expert (for filings and deductions)
- A mentor (for strategy, confidence, and connections)

These people don't cost you money—they save you money, time, and stress.

*As a member of the **Ten 7** team, you will have access to informational videos at* https://goten7.com *from our attorneys, tax experts, and mentors that will give you much needed backup in your business.*

Tool 6: Your Business Identity

Don't underestimate the importance of branding—even on day one.

One of the greatest advantages my business experience gave me when I was elected sheriff was the understanding of the importance of branding. Your ability to brand yourself, your business, or your products will drive your success.

While my drive to brand my agency and myself often made my command staff and county uncomfortable, it's what drove our success. Our branding made us successful in the law enforcement market for hiring. Our sheriff's office is on the outskirts of the Phoenix Valley, so we had to compete with a lot of big, shiny, high-paying law enforcement agencies. Not only did we compete, but we were dominating. Both new cadets and lateral officers sought out our agency because of the branding. We managed to brand ourselves as an agency where you could still be a cop, and we protected our people.

Branding also put us on the map nationally. On social media, we were number two in the nation, only behind the FBI, for Facebook followers. I'm not aware of any agency that has more YouTube followers than our agency had. All of that national branding gave us the leverage to build our agency and get our troops raise after raise.

Branding is your identity. Branding is your power. Branding is everything. Brand yourself and your business in a way that everybody knows who you are, what your business does, and that you're the best at what you do.

At Ten 7 we will help you come up with a branding strategy for success. Membership in Ten 7 will provide you with more in-depth information and support to help you define your identity and brand, but here a few key steps:

- **Choose a business name** that's easy to remember and reflects what you do.
- **Secure a domain name** and social media handles to match.
- **Get a logo**—even a simple one—so you look professional and trustworthy.

Optional but helpful: Consider registering a trademark or filing a DBA (Doing Business As) if your business name differs from your legal structure.

For more information about branding, choosing a business name, securing a domain, and getting a logo for your business, please join the **Ten 7** *community at* https://goten7.com *for complete videos from our experts. Our legal team specializes in trademarks, patents, and copyrights as well.*

A Story: The Power of Presentation

A buddy of mine launched a home security company. Great experience, amazing service, but no website, no logo, and his business cards looked like they were made on a typewriter.

He was losing leads—not because of skill, but because people didn't trust what they couldn't see.

Once he cleaned up his branding—professional logo, sharp website, solid messaging—his conversions doubled. Same guy. Same service. Just a better toolkit.

Present yourself and your business for success.

Tool 7: Your Insurance and Protection

In law enforcement, you wouldn't hit the road without body armor. Don't run your business without protection either.

- **General liability insurance** protects you from injuries, property damage, or lawsuits.
- **Professional liability** is useful if you give advice, coaching, or consultations.
- **Cybersecurity tools**—even free or low-cost options—are essential if you're collecting customer info online.

Peace of mind is part of your business strategy.

Tool 8: Your Mission Brief

In law enforcement, you had a mission brief before hitting the street. Same in business. Write down your mission:

- What does your business do?
- Who do you serve?
- What problem are you solving?
- What makes you different?

This becomes your North Star for every decision you make.

Checkpoint: Build Your Toolkit

- Have I chosen my business structure (LLC, sole prop, etc.)?

  * We can help you at *https://goten7.com*

- Have I filed for my EIN?

  * We can help you at *https://goten7.com*

- Do I have a separate business bank account?

  * We can help you at *https://goten7.com*

- Am I tracking income and expenses clearly?

  * We can help you at *https://goten7.com*

- Do I have a basic system to contact, invoice, and serve clients?

  * We can help you at *https://goten7.com*

- Do I have legal and financial advisors I trust?

  * We can help you at *https://goten7.com*

- Do I have a clear brand and mission statement?

  * We can help you at *https://goten7.com*

- Have I protected myself with insurance and security tools?

  * We can help you at *https://goten7.com*

If you're missing a few of these, that's okay. We can help you at *https://goten7.com*. You've worn gear your whole life. Now it's time to gear up for your business—properly, legally, and powerfully.

The mission can't succeed without the right tools. This mission will struggle to succeed without **Ten 7.**

PART III
Leading Beyond the Line

CHAPTER TEN

Traffic, Trauma, and Triggers

*You've earned the right to prioritize
what matters most. This chapter is about
boundaries, ownership of time, and legacy.*

You've seen more in one career than most people will in a lifetime.

You've zipped up body bags. Held broken families together at crash scenes. Had weapons pointed at you. Been cursed, blamed, spat on—and kept going.

You may not be aware of the following statistic about law enforcement and the policing profession—I know I wasn't when I heard it several years ago. I was aware police officers are exposed to lots of stresses and may get injured, but I didn't realize to what extent.

A study done in 2021 by the Avon and Somerset Police Federation found that the average police officer, during their career, will experience four hundred to seven hundred potentially traumatic events where the average citizen will only experience two to four. That is an eye-popping statistic. It is also very telling of what we see and go through during our careers.

To effectively process what we experience, we learn to compartmentalize. To "deal with it later." But here's the truth: Later is now.

You're stepping into a new chapter. And if you don't face what's inside the box, or like I mentioned in chapter one, that closet we stuff everything into, it can and will show up in your business, your family, and your future.

Let Go of the Nostalgia

We don't talk about the emotional residue of service. I honestly don't know if talking about it is the right fix.

I, like most law enforcement and military, am not a touchy-feely guy. I don't believe in talking to a therapist or trauma dumping on somebody. I have found my peace through God first and foremost. I have also found peace through serving others and working hard on projects that give me purpose. I have found work to be very therapeutic for me. I have found my escape in starting and building businesses.

The traffic stop that went sideways. The child you couldn't save. The friend you lost in the line of duty or in the combat zone. The guilt, the adrenaline, the constant scanning of rooms.

You carry that stuff with you, even after the badge comes off. While you can talk about it or try to forget it, there is one thing that is certain: You can't erase the past or what you've experienced.

I have found this to be the key for me. My full understanding of the eternal fact that you cannot change the past keeps me from trying to explain my losses, revel in my victories, feel guilt for the outcomes I erroneously thought I could change, complain about my past conditions or circumstances, or be nostalgic about who I was or what I did.

One characteristic found in multimillionaires is they are not nostalgic. They are not nostalgic for the past, bad or good, and they are not ruminating on the future. They live in the now and understand the past is the past, the future is uncertain, and the here and now is what matters. Too many people are haunted by their past experiences or long for their past successes. That's nostalgia. Too many people also are scared of a future that hasn't happened and will most likely never happen, or they long for a better future. That's rumination.

What are you doing today? Today matters.

During my time as sheriff, we sought out many different programs and products that would help officer wellness. We owed it to our employees, their families, and the community to ensure their wellness was being addressed. We wanted to know: How could we help them process the traumatic events they have seen and would see? How could we help them sleep better? How could we reduce alcohol or substance dependency or abuse among our men and women? How could we improve their home and family life?

One of the most successful wellness programs we implemented was called Vitanya. It was so successful that after retiring, I sought out Vitanya as a potential client for my consulting business.

To simplify what Vitanya is, it's a brain mapping program. As you can imagine, police officers and military are very reluctant to try new things, especially something like this where you place your hand on a sensor and the program begins to map your brain. Vitanya then creates a plan to realign things in your brain. I can imagine what you are thinking even just reading this. For that reason, my chiefs, a few members of my command staff, and I would do the program first to lead by example.

Here is what we saw. All of us were seasoned law enforcement, with years of experiences, stress, and trauma.

Most of us were struggling with getting good sleep, irritability, and daily stress. Some of the command staff were even seriously considering retirement because they had lost their passion for the job.

The program takes about six months; however, we started to see the positive results within weeks. We all started to sleep better and deeper, with good dreams. The others and I immediately became less irritable. And over time I began to forget the traumatic events. Even if I did remember them, they conjured up no feelings.

To this day I attribute my positive mental and health wellness in large part to Vitanya. Here is the craziest part: no medication, no trauma dumping, no therapist, just rewiring and remapping the brain.

Whatever path you choose to address the traumatic events of your career, make sure it starts with God. And remember, you can't change the past. Everything that has happened to you is simply life and for your benefit.

A Story: The One That Crushed Me

Oddly enough, the most traumatic, most crushing experience of my law enforcement career had nothing to do with policing, however it would change my life and my family's lives forever.

I'm going share a couple of personal stories with you. I have five children. My middle son, Cooper, when he was fourteen or fifteen, started hanging around the wrong people, got into drugs, and eventually even started getting into fentanyl. Over the years his substance abuse was getting worse and worse. His behavior caused us to prohibit him from driving any of our cars.

One evening we went to a charity event. While at the charity event I got a phone call from my son, Cooper, who said, "Dad, I just hit a guy on a bike." This was not good at all. One of our worst fears had just smacked us right in the face. We hustled out of the charity event and drove over to where he was.

When we got to the scene, not far from our house, I got out of the car and checked on my son. I looked at him and asked, "Hey, you okay?" He said he was. Then I walked over to the bike rider lying on the dirt, just at the edge of the roadway, where the firefighters were working on him. He didn't look good. While I stood there, I was just praying he wouldn't die, because if he died, we'd have problems. We had big problems anyway, but a fatality would have been terrible for the victim, his family, and my son.

I walked back to my son, who was standing there surrounded by a handful of deputies, and had to do one of the hardest things I've ever done in my entire life. I looked him in the eye and I said, "I have to leave you here. If I stay here, they're going to say that I influenced this case in some way. You're on your own."

I think he was eighteen or nineteen at the time.

One of hardest things to do was to walk away from him, get in my car, and drive away. The guilt we felt, leaving him standing there, was heavy. I think he was angry and felt betrayed by us for a long time after that, but we had to let him deal with the consequences of his decisions.

Fortunately, the guy did not die.

While that moment didn't end my son's struggles with drugs, he did eventually have his wake-up moment and went cold turkey from fentanyl and drugs.

He had been clean about a year and a half, but he ended up doing six months in my jail for hitting the guy on the bike. He finished his six-month sentence in October of 2022.

Fast-forward to December of 2022, and he was doing great. He had a fiancée. His beautiful baby girl was eleven months old. He had a good job. Life was good for him.

On Friday, December 16, 2022, around eight thirty at night, we got a knock on the door that would change our lives forever.

We opened the door and standing there was the sheriff from the neighboring county, two of my chiefs, and two guys from Gilbert PD. And my chief, who's known my kids since they were little, just looked at me, overcome with emotion and barely able to speak. All he could say was, "Cooper and the baby are dead."

In an instant, I lost my twenty-two-year-old son, my eleven-month-old granddaughter, and my soon-to-be daughter-in-law, who died a few days later from her injuries. The three of them were taken from us in the blink of an eye. Taken by a careless young man driving under the influence of alcohol and drugs.

We were crushed! We didn't even want to get out of bed. We were shells of ourselves. Nothing else seemed to be of any importance. We were completely numb.

About a month after the funeral, we were still in a fog of depression and grief. One day, while we were hollowly going about our upturned lives, somebody said something to us. I don't remember what it was, but just like that, boom, it sparked us back in. The fog lifted.

I looked at my wife and we knew immediately what we had to do. Snapping out of the haze of depression reminded us there is no guarantee for tomorrow, and the only thing you take with you in this life is what you do. So we looked at the experience of losing our kids and said, "We're gonna get up," "We're gonna dust ourselves off," "We're gonna move forward," and "We're gonna do what the Lord's asking us to do."

That moment changed how I led, how I loved—and how I healed.

Mental Toughness vs. Emotional Avoidance

Being tough isn't about never crying or never struggling. Being tough is about facing the hard stuff—and doing the work anyway. Pulling up your bootstraps, dusting yourself off, and moving forward.

For so many years it was a black mark on our careers if we showed any kind of weakness. Thankfully those times are changing.

What my family and I experienced when we lost our kids was tough. It was also very public. I'm not sure whether the publicity made it easier or harder. While we didn't have to battle the emotions in private or on our own, we also had to address it over and over again in public. For years, everywhere we went, because it was so public, we had the wound reopened. It was nice knowing people cared so much about us, but it also kept it fresh on our hearts and minds every time somebody would express their condolences. This went on for years.

I was also running for the US Senate in Arizona, so instead of avoiding this tragic and public experience for our family, we leaned into it. We found purpose in our tragedy. We used it as drive. We embraced the trauma and let it strengthen us.

What we realized is everyone has been through or is going through a tough time. You are not alone. When you realize that, it has a way of consoling you and freeing you from feeling traumatized or alone. Think of those experiences as being what creates the superhero in you. Whatever you do, don't let it make you a villain.

A Story from the Front Seat

I remember sitting in the emergency room watching a high school friend and her husband crying, completely devastated.

Just an hour before, I was the first on the scene of an accident involving a motorcycle and a vehicle. My first visual was of a young man lying lifeless on the street. I immediately began performing CPR. As other deputies and rescue services began to show up and assist in life-saving measures, it was clear to me that this young man may not make it. I could see he lived nearby, so I decided to make sure his parents and family knew what was going on.

I arrived at the residence of the young man, heart heavy, hat in hand. I'm sure my face said everything. The young man's father answered the door. He gave me a friendly greeting, but my demeanor quickly changed the mood. I told him his son had been involved in a serious accident and was in very critical condition. He went back in the house to get his wife. It wasn't until then that my friend, who I hadn't seen since high school, came out the door crying and embraced me. I can still hear her saying, "Oh, Mark!" I had no idea this was her son.

I escorted them to the hospital and into the emergency room.

Unfortunately, as I stood there silently in the emergency room with the family, they were given the life-altering news by the doctors that their son had passed away from his injuries.

While my heart was truly broken for them, I didn't fully grasp their pain and trauma until about six months later, when I received the same devastating knock at the door with the news that I had lost my children. The pain of losing a loved one unexpectedly is deep, but the pain of losing a child is crushing.

For us in law enforcement, fire rescue, and military, these are the calls, the moments we see that change us in a way that we don't truly understand. We are often seen as heroes in other people's lives, but most of the time those experiences or calls leave us feeling more hollow than heroic.

We're taught to brush it off. "Just another day" or "just another call." But it's not. Every one of those scenes leaves a mark. You can't change it. You can't outrun it. You have to outwork it.

Simple Practices for Mental Strength

You don't need to do anything silly like sit cross-legged and meditate for hours. Start here:

- Schedule quiet time daily. Even ten minutes with no phone, no noise.
- Write it out. A few lines a day in a notebook about what you're thinking, feeling, remembering.
- Talk to someone. A friend. A chaplain. A professional. Someone who understands the weight.
- Move your body. Exercise isn't just for strength, it's for sanity.
- Check your fuel. What you eat, drink, and consume (online and off) directly affects your mindset.
- Work. Stay busy. Start a business. Do something that takes away from the boredom.
- Develop rituals that ground you—morning walks, evening gratitude lists, prayer, or scripture.

A Word on Triggers

Triggers aren't just emotional. They're physical. They're real.

Smells, sounds, even lighting can transport you back to scenes you'd rather forget. And sometimes, the people around you don't understand why you "overreact."

These triggers don't mean you're crazy or weak. They just mean you are human.

That's why awareness matters. When you know what sets you off, you can build better responses.

You're not trying to be perfect. You're trying to stay present.

Checkpoint: Emotional Inventory

Answer these in a quiet moment—honestly:

- What's one call, deployment, or memory that still haunts me?
- How do I typically respond when I feel overwhelmed or triggered?
- What haven't I said out loud that's been building inside me?
- Who could I talk to about this, and what's stopping me?
- What healthy habits have helped me stay grounded in the past?

You've led through gunfire and grief. Now it's time to lead yourself into peace, purpose, and prosperity.

Healing isn't a detour from the mission—it *is* the mission.

CHAPTER ELEVEN

One Bite at a Time

Encouraging readers to give back—hire fellow veterans, mentor new entrepreneurs, volunteer. The mission grows.

There's a saying you've probably heard: "How do you eat an elephant? One bite at a time."

Starting a business—or rebuilding your life after decades of structure, adrenaline, and high-stakes leadership—can feel overwhelming.

You look at the to-do list, the ideas, the fears, the unknowns...and it feels like you've been served an entire elephant and all you have to eat it with is a plastic fork.

This can be especially difficult if you don't know even the most basic steps of starting a new business, let alone operating that business and having success. That overwhelming feeling can be scary and even paralyzing.

The key is not to think about having to eat the "whole elephant." Start with one bite. Start by taking one step.

There is a quote I love from a book called *The Boy, the Mole, the Fox and the Horse.* "I can't see a way through," said the boy. "Can you see your next step?" asked the horse. The boy replied, "Yes," and the horse said, "Just take that."

This quote is a simple reminder that when you are feeling overwhelmed, focus on the present moment and take small steps forward. One bite at a time.

When I decided to run for sheriff, I was embarking on something about which I had no idea what I was doing. I was overwhelmed with all of the things I had to do to officially be a candidate. Plus, I was running a business, so you can only imagine the weight on my shoulders. One of the things I would consistently tell myself was, "One bite at a time, Mark, one bite at a time."

There is a saying, "Be careful what you wish for, you just might get it all." I eventually ate that elephant of running a business and a sheriff's race at the same time, when I won. Winning didn't make the overwhelming feeling go away, it compounded it. As the sheriff, I felt like I was faced with eating two elephants. You know how you eat two elephants? One bite at a time.

The more you push yourself, the more you challenge yourself and the more you want from life. I can assure you of one thing: You will feel overwhelmed.

Starting and running a business will make you feel overwhelmed. Just eat that elephant one bite at a time.

The good news? The Ten 7 community will help you eat that elephant. Let our experts and staff at Ten 7 help you take those bites.

Here is some more good news: You've climbed mountains before. And every time, it started the same way: one foot in front of the other. If you can see your next step, just take that one.

One bite at a time.

You Don't Need to Have It All Figured Out

When you were on patrol, you didn't always know how the call would unfold. You just knew how to start.

When you were in the military, you didn't know every mission detail, but you trusted the plan, the training, and the next step.

That same principle applies to your business.

You don't need:

- A full website

- Ten clients
- A complete product
- A bank loan

You just need a direction and a decision. Then you move.

Having said that, business can go a lot smoother when you do have a website, clients, complete products, or the finances to market your product or services. That's where being a member of **Ten 7** can help.

The Power of Daily Progress

Want to know the real secret to success?

Consistency beats intensity.

- Ten pushups every day beats 100 once a month.
- $1 saved every day beats $100 once a year.
- One hour focused on your business every morning beats twelve-hour bursts followed by burnout.
- Small wins, stacked daily, create massive results.

In 1998, I left a safe and consistent but limited-growth job to drive across the country to Tampa, Florida for a door-to-door sales job. I had my wife, who was eight months pregnant, and a two-year-old son, and I was jumping off the edge of comfort into the turbulent and risky world of sales.

Several years earlier, while serving as a missionary in Argentina, I had done a lot of door-to-door work, but I had never sold anything door-to-door. Now I was going to stake my family's well-being on being able to sell pest control door-to-door.

I enthusiastically hit the doors on day one, only to come home at the end of a very long day with zero sales. If memory serves me correctly, I was the only one from our sales team without a sale.

Day two, another long day on the doors...zero sales.

Day three, another goose egg. What made it even harder was that everybody else was racking up sales.

Day four, a long day of busting my butt, from one house to the next, pitch after pitch. The result: zero sales.

I can still remember the feelings of doubt and despair. I asked my wife, "Did I make the wrong decision in coming out here?" "Was my family right about this not being the right thing to do?" "Am I just not good at sales?" These questions and so many others clattered around in my brain.

In all the anxiety and uncertainty, I decided there was only one thing to do: be consistent. Just keep consistently grinding away every day. I was confident that the consistent hard work had no other outcome but success. So that's what I did.

Day five, after another consistent day of work, four sales. Boom! The consistent work paid off.

That summer I was the most consistent salesman of the team. I didn't have the record for the most sales in a day, and I was the last guy to get on the sales board, but by the end of the summer I was by far the leading salesman for the summer.

I applied consistency over intensity. Every day I worked. Every day I grinded. Every day I was consistent.

I have taken that same consistent approach to my work and businesses. No matter how bad a day, or two days, or four days can be, I learned that consistent effort and work would produce positive results.

Later, when I started my own pest control company, I didn't launch it with a staff or a marketing team. I launched it at my kitchen table, driving a beat-up truck, and with a list of five people I knew. I called them. I followed up. I stayed consistent.

Three of them became clients. The rest referred me to others. Momentum starts small and builds when you stay committed.

Your Mission Plan: Bite by Bite

Here's a simple weekly rhythm to gain momentum:

- Monday: Vision and Planning – What are this week's priorities?
- Tuesday: Outreach – Who can I serve, contact, or follow up with?
- Wednesday: Creation – Build the thing: the course, product, service.
- Thursday: Operations – Emails, legal, systems, admin.
- Friday: Reflection – What worked? What didn't? What's next?

Even sixty to ninety minutes per day following that rhythm will change your trajectory in ninety days.

A Lesson from the Field

When I was going through the police academy, they didn't teach us everything in a day. It was one block at a time. Physical fitness, then report writing, then firearms, then driving, then use of force, then law. Piece by piece. One skill built on top of another.

Then, when we were done with the academy, we started our field training. It was overwhelming, but we tackled one call at a time. One traffic stop at a time. One arrest at a time. One report at a time. Nobody expected us to be perfect. Our FTOs (Field Training Officers) expected us to show up, be consistent, be confident, make decisions, learn from our mistakes, and get better.

No matter what you do, no one expects you to be an expert on day one. They just expect you to commit to the process.

Business works the same way. Each day, you learn a little more. You refine. You adjust. You get sharper. That's how you win.

Don't Be Afraid to Start Small

Too often, we get paralyzed by perfection. We wait until the logo is perfect, the plan is airtight, the website is ready.

But here's what I've learned: Clarity comes through movement, not meditation.

A really great book that I highly recommend is *You²*. The book talks about taking "quantum leaps" in life, and one of the chapters is "Make your move before you're ready."

That chapter talks about not getting bogged down in getting prepared for what you want to do. Whatever you need will come as you go. You'll also discover, once you are underway, that you know more than you think you know.

That chapter also mentions how crucial of an element mobility is.

I remember when I was going through SWAT school, they would teach you the difference between concealment and cover. It was very easy to get comfortable behind the perceived safety of the cover. Then you would hear the instructor shout, "Move!" It's not always easy, but you have to move. You have to trust your instincts.

One of my favorite lines from that chapter is: "'Getting ready' is, quite frankly, a stalling tactic, an act of anxiety, a con game you're working on yourself."

If you are waiting for the stars to align, for perfection, for the "right time," you will be waiting for a very long time and your business will most likely never get off the ground. No matter how great your service, product, or idea is, if you don't move, it will fail.

Start small. Take one step, then another. As you move you will figure things out. Your gut instincts will carry you through. You will consistently get better and you will see success.

You figure things out by doing, not by overthinking.

Your first version won't be your best version, but it will be your most important. Because it gets you in the game.

▌Checkpoint: Bite-Sized Action

Ask yourself:

- What's one small action I can take today to move my business forward?

- What's one habit I could commit to for the next thirty days?
- What's been paralyzing me, and how can I take the first bite?

Write down those answers. Circle one. Do it today.

Final Thought

You don't need a feast. You just need a fork.

This next chapter of your life doesn't get built overnight. It gets built brick by brick, bite by bite, call by call.

You've already proven you're willing to show up. Now show up for yourself.

The mission ahead may be different, but your tools haven't changed: grit, discipline, faith, courage.

Keep going. One bite at a time.

CHAPTER TWELVE

Ten 7 Forever

*A final charge. Just as you ended your career
with a "Ten 7," this new mission begins with it.
It's not the end—it's the call to a new beginning.*

The last time I picked up the radio, you could tell in my voice I was doing everything I could to hold back emotion.

It wasn't fear—it was finality. Eight years. Two terms. Hundreds of deputies. Thousands of calls. One community I'd bled for, fought for, loved deeply.

I looked out at the sea of patrol vehicles lining the streets. Helicopter above. My chief deputy behind the wheel. My wife, kids, and grandkids in the driveway.

And I spoke the words I'll never forget:

"Pinal 1... I just want to say thank you to all the dispatchers, the deputies, the detention officers, the employees, the posse, the COPs (Citizens on Patrol), and especially my command staff. Thank you for a great eight years. It's been an honor to serve with you. I love every one of you. I'm going to miss you a ton. Pinal 1 signing off for the last time. Please show me Ten 7."

Even though that was the end of my time as sheriff and my law enforcement career, it also represented the beginning of a new and exciting life.

The Shift Ends. The Mission Begins. Your Life Begins.

For years, "Ten 7" meant you were out of service. End of the shift. Off-duty. Done for the day. Now it means something more. It means you're off their clock but finally on your own. It's the beginning of a whole new life.

You've stepped out of the uniform, but not out of purpose. You've handed in your badge, but not your identity. You've closed a chapter—but you're writing a new one.

And the best part: This time, you hold the pen.

You're not waiting for the next shift, you're building it. You're not chasing a paycheck, you're creating a legacy.

The world still needs you. However, now it needs what only you can bring. Your scars. Your experience. Your values. Your leadership.

What Legacy Will You Build?

The job gave you stories. Now it's time to turn those stories into something that lasts.

- A business your kids can inherit.
- A book that inspires the next generation.
- A brand that echoes your values.
- A community that supports warriors like you.
- A homestead, a movement, a mission.

You've already lived for others. Now live for impact.

For two decades I put on a uniform, a badge, and I went to work. Every day and every call for service, I was there to help other people. Every day I would kiss my wife, say goodbye to my kids, and walk out the door, there was a strong chance I would be injured or maybe even killed in the line of duty. I did it so I could help others in their worst moments, or so maybe I could have a positive impact on somebody's life. I lived for others.

Then I was elected sheriff. Living for and serving other people went to a whole other level as the elected sheriff. Every day I spent valuable time and energy serving the needs of my community. I also put my whole heart and mind into my employees and their families. My family and I risked everything for others. We risked our reputations to defend the freedoms and constitutional rights of others.

Politics is not for the faint of heart. While the office of sheriff is a law enforcement position, it is still a political office. As if the county politics weren't bad enough, I decided to take on a statewide political race. Why? I didn't need a job. I loved being the sheriff. So why would I make the decision to run for the US Senate, knowing how time-consuming it would be, knowing how ugly the politics would be, and knowing that, win or lose, I would have to retire from being the sheriff, a job I loved.

Why? Because I have a heart for service. I could see there was a need to fight for our country and our freedoms and to serve in a different arena.

As a county sheriff, I could protect my herd from the wolves. However, I also knew that if somebody didn't actively hunt those wolves, they would eventually multiply, and even the best of the sheepdogs wouldn't be able to stop them from wreaking havoc on our herds. Somebody needed to step up and hunt those wolves out in Washington, DC.

It's not in my nature to stand on the corner and watch the building burn to the ground. It's not in my nature to watch the wolf ravage the sheep either. What kind of man would I be if I stood there and waited for somebody else to run into that burning building or stop the wolf from destroying the sheep?

My desire to serve others, to serve my country, drove me to make that jump into the Senate race, regardless of the consequences.

And what were the consequences? I lost the Senate race and I had to retire. People often ask me if I regret running for Senate, and my answer is always, "No." I was in the arena. My face was marred by dust and sweat and blood, but I stayed in the arena. A true servant is willing to risk it all.

The other thing that people ask me now is if I will run for office again. The truth is, I honestly don't know. What I do know is, I have served. I have lived for others over and over again. I have staked everything, including my life, for others. Now I will live for impact, and so should you.

Just like me, you have lived for others. Whether you were a first responder or in the military, you served and lived for others. Here's the mission now: Make an impact on your family's lives and on your life, and by doing so, you will find a way to impact others as well.

You've spent decades proving yourself to others. Now it's time to prove to yourself that you're more than just the badge.

You've carried others. Now it's time to build something that carries your name.

A Story: The Last Day, the First Step

After I signed off, I hugged my family. I stood in my driveway and looked at the patrol vehicles as they slowly pulled away.

For the first time in a long time, there was silence.

I didn't have the radio buzzing. I didn't have 600 employees relying on my decisions. The weight lifted, but so did the structure.

The next morning, I woke up and realized: This is the first day of the rest of my life. And what I do from here...is entirely up to me.

That is liberating for all of us, but also terrifying for some of you. It's okay to feel that way.

We created **Ten 7** to help you feel less terrified. To help you transition. To help you truly take advantage of your liberation.

You are free!

The morning after I retired, here is what I reminded myself: I've never backed down from a challenge, and I wasn't about to start now.

This Is the New Beat

Entrepreneur. Mentor. Patriot. Builder. Warrior in a new arena.

This is your next shift. Your next badge. Your next "call sign."

And you're not alone.

We're here. The Ten 7 community is here. Other brothers and sisters who've made the leap. Who are fighting for their families, their freedom, and their future—just like you.

We've got your six.

You served your country. Now serve your family, your calling, and your purpose.

Final Checkpoint: Your Commissioning

Write this down, say it out loud—make it yours:

- I am not retired. I am redeployed.
- My life has meaning beyond the uniform.
- My experience is valuable. My pain is fuel.
- I will build boldly. Serve deeply. Lead with purpose.
- I am not done. I'm just getting started.
- I am Ten 7—forever.

Final Word: Lamb Out

You answered the call for years. You led from the front. You served with honor.

Now, brother—now, sister—it's time to lead yourself.

Pick up your gear. Open that business. Mentor that next warrior. And keep showing up—every single day.

When we say, "Ten 7," it doesn't mean you're done.

It means this is "when your shift ends and your life begins."

Let's go kick some a**!

Please show me **Ten 7**!